University Success

LISTENING AND SPEAKING

BEGINNING

Cynthia Fettig

University Success Listening and Speaking, Beginning

Copyright © 2020 by Pearson Education, Inc.

All rights reserved.

Pearson Education, 221 River Street, Hoboken, NJ 07030

Staff credits: The people who made up the *University Success* team, representing content development, design, multimedia, project management, publishing, and rights management are Pietro Alongi, Sheila Ameri, Stephanie Callahan, Tracey Cataldo, Dave Dickey, Gina DiLillo, Warren Fischbach, Sarah Henrich, Niki Lee, Agnieszka Leszkiewicz, Amy McCormick, Robert Ruvo, Katarzyna Starzynska-Kosciuszko, Paula Van Ells, and Joseph Vella.

Project management: Debbie Sistino

Instructional Design: Tim McLaughlin

MyEnglishLab author: Amy Renehan

Contributing editors: Eleanor Kirby Barnes, Linda Butler, Jaimie Scanlon, Leigh Stolle, and Sarah Wales-McGrath

Video development: Christen L. Savage

Video production: ITN Productions

Text composition: EMC Design Ltd

Library of Congress Cataloging-in-Publication Data

A catalog record for the print edition is available from the Library of Congress.

Printed in the United States of America

ISBN 10: 0-13-524594-X

ISBN 13: 978-0-13-524594-1

1 2019

Contents

Welcome to *University Success*

INTRODUCTION

University Success is a five-level academic series designed to equip beginning through transition level English learners with the language skills necessary to succeed in university courses. At the upper levels, the three strands, Reading, Writing, and Oral Communication, are fully aligned across content and skills and provide students with an inspiring collection of extensive authentic content. The series has been developed in cooperation with subject matter experts, all thought leaders in their fields. The upper levels are organized around five distinct content areas—The Human Experience, Money and Commerce, The Science of Nature, Arts and Letters, and Structural Science. By focusing on STEAM topics, *University Success* helps equip students with the critical thinking skills and creative innovation necessary for success in their future careers.

University Success levels from Intermediate to Transition model the type of real-life learning situations that students face when studying for a degree. The lower levels, Beginning and High-Beginning, lay the groundwork and build the support that students need to prepare them for the complexity and challenge of the upper levels.

BUILDING THE FOUNDATION

Beginning students face a daunting challenge as they build the English-language skills needed for academic success. The Beginning and High-Beginning levels support these students by providing the scaffolding to construct a strong linguistic core. The two integrated skills strands (Reading and Writing and Listening and Speaking) include four distinct content areas that link to the content areas of the *University Success* upper levels. This allows students to build a background in basic concepts and vocabulary in these STEAM content areas: Business, Humanities, Structural Science, and Natural Science. These levels fuse high-interest, engaging content with carefully scaffolded tasks to develop the language skills needed for managing complex and conceptually challenging content.

Task types are recycled across content areas to reinforce skills and give students the confidence they need to take on ever-more challenging material. By using Bloom's Taxonomy as a framework, *University Success* strongly emphasizes the learning process. The series's targeted approach to vocabulary instruction includes both academic and high-frequency vocabulary and provides the basic building blocks needed to construct meaningful speech and writing. A variety of level-appropriate input, as well as visuals, organizers, and critical thinking and discussion activities enable students to fully internalize the content and solidify their linguistic foundation.

TWO STRANDS SUPPORT THE PATH TO LEARNER AUTONOMY

The two lower-level strands are fully aligned across content areas and skills, allowing teachers to utilize material from different strands to support learning. The strands are complementary, providing the teacher with aligned content across all four skills to be utilized in an integrated skills classroom. This allows students to build a solid background in basic concepts and vocabulary in each of the four content areas.

BEGINNING LEVEL

CEFR **A1**   GSE **22–32**

READING AND WRITING

Architecture

Genetics
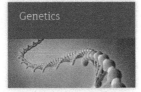

Business and Technology

Psychology

SKILLS

- Identify the main idea
- Understand compare and contrast
- Express likes and preferences
- Write basic descriptions
- Write basic directions

LISTENING AND SPEAKING

Architecture

Genetics

Business and Technology

Psychology

SKILLS

- Understand the gist
- Identify compare and contrast signposts
- Express likes and preferences
- Describe people, places, and things
- Give basic instructions

HIGH-BEGINNING LEVEL

CEFR **A2–A2+**   GSE **33–42**

READING AND WRITING

Money and E-Commerce

Cultural Anthropology

Civil Engineering

Sustainable Agriculture

SKILLS

- Preview and predict
- Scan for details
- Recognize narratives
- Follow steps in a process
- Write a simple story
- Describe visuals

LISTENING AND SPEAKING

Money and E-Commerce

Cultural Anthropology

Civil Engineering

Sustainable Agriculture

SKILLS

- Predict
- Listen for details
- Identify events in a narrative
- Understand steps in a process
- Tell a story
- Describe objects

BUILDING THE FOUNDATION FOR *UNIVERSITY SUCCESS*

Two integrated-skills strands with explicit skill development tied to specific learning outcomes establish the foundation for higher-level academic success.

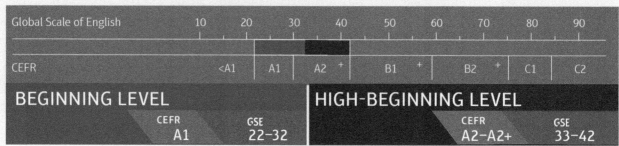

BEGINNING LEVEL

CEFR A1 **GSE** 22–32

The Beginning level gives students the fundamental building blocks and confidence to take on academic challenges.

INTENSIVE SKILL PRACTICE

Intensive skill practice tied to learning objectives informed by the Global Scale of English

ACADEMIC HIGH-INTEREST CONTENT

- Academic content linked to STEAM disciplines provides a bridge to the upper levels.
- Introducing each unit is a video featuring an overview of the academic area.
- High-interest topics and a variety of genres increase motivation.
- Two chapters within each content unit include recycled tasks and vocabulary and give students a solid background in basic concepts.

SCAFFOLDED APPROACH

- Chapters are heavily scaffolded with multiple guided exercises that follow Bloom's Taxonomy as a framework.
- Prediction and skill comprehension tasks accompany each reading and listening.
- Step-by-step application of all productive skills is practiced throughout each chapter.
- Readings and listenings are "chunked" and include accompanying visuals.
- Extensive integration of graphic organizers is included.

EXPLICIT VOCABULARY INSTRUCTION

A targeted approach to vocabulary including
- contextualized previews with pronunciation practice
- reviews in the Student Book and in MyEnglishLab
- collaborative tasks
- vocabulary tips
- a vocabulary building and expansion section
- an end-of-chapter vocabulary checklist

GRAMMAR FOR WRITING / SPEAKING

A dedicated grammar presentation with controlled practice tasks in the Student Book and in MyEnglishLab provide scaffolding for the writing and speaking tasks.

SOFT SKILLS

Task-based strategies linked to chapter topics focus on academic success, life skills, and college readiness.

HIGH-BEGINNING LEVEL

CEFR A2–A2+ **GSE** 33–42

The High-Beginning level builds the support that prepares students for the rigor and challenges of the upper levels and beyond.

INTENSIVE SKILL PRACTICE

Intensive skill practice tied to learning objectives informed by the Global Scale of English

ACADEMIC HIGH-INTEREST CONTENT

- Academic content linked to STEAM disciplines provides a bridge to the upper levels.
- Introducing each unit is a video featuring a university professor, which gives students an academic perspective.
- High-interest topics and a variety of genres increase motivation.
- Two chapters within each content unit include recycled tasks and vocabulary and give students a solid background in academic concepts.

SCAFFOLDED APPROACH

- Chapters are carefully scaffolded with multiple guided exercises that follow Bloom's Taxonomy as a framework.
- Practical application of all productive skills is integrated in every chapter.
- Readings and listenings are "chunked," with skill and comprehension tasks integrated throughout.
- Extensive use of graphic organizers aids in note-taking.

EXPLICIT VOCABULARY INSTRUCTION

A targeted approach to vocabulary including
- vocabulary tasks pre- and post-reading and listening
- vocabulary tips and glossing of receptive vocabulary
- a vocabulary strategy section in every chapter
- online reviews with pronunciation practice

GRAMMAR FOR WRITING / SPEAKING

- A dedicated grammar presentation prepares students for authentic writing and speaking tasks.
- Grammar practices in the Student Book and in MyEnglishLab move from controlled to practical application.

SOFT SKILLS

Task-based strategies linked to chapter topics focus on academic success, life skills, and college readiness.

PUTTING STUDENTS ON THE PATH TO *UNIVERSITY SUCCESS*

Intensive skill development and extended application—tied to specific learning outcomes—provide the scaffolding English language learners need to become confident and successful in a university setting.

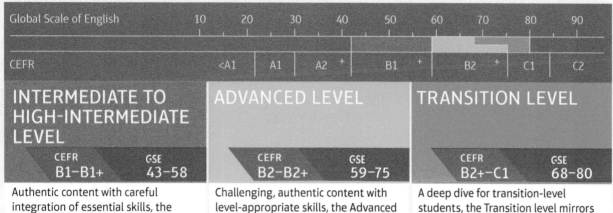

Global Scale of English	10	20	30	40	50	60	70	80	90
CEFR		<A1	A1	A2 +	B1 +	B2 +	C1	C2

INTERMEDIATE TO HIGH-INTERMEDIATE LEVEL

CEFR B1–B1+ **GSE** 43–58

Authentic content with careful integration of essential skills, the Intermediate to High-Intermediate level familiarizes students with real-world academic contexts.

INTENSIVE SKILL PRACTICE

Intensive skill practice tied to learning objectives informed by the Global Scale of English

AUTHENTIC CONTENT

- Readings: 200–2,000 words
- Lectures: 15–20 minutes
- Multiple exposures and chunking

EXPLICIT VOCABULARY INSTRUCTION

- Pre- and post-reading and listening vocabulary tasks
- Glossing of receptive vocabulary
- Recycling throughout each part and online

SCAFFOLDED APPROACH

Multiple guided exercises focus on comprehension, application, and clarification of productive skills.

VOCABULARY STRATEGIES

Vocabulary strategy sections focus on form, use, and meaning.

GRAPHIC ORGANIZERS

Extensive integration of graphic organizers throughout to support note-taking and help students process complex content.

ADVANCED LEVEL

CEFR B2–B2+ **GSE** 59–75

Challenging, authentic content with level-appropriate skills, the Advanced level prepares students to exit the ESL safety net.

INTENSIVE SKILL PRACTICE

Intensive skill practice tied to learning objectives informed by the Global Scale of English

AUTHENTIC CONTENT

- Readings: 200–3,000 words
- Lectures: 20 minutes

EXPLICIT VOCABULARY INSTRUCTION

- Pre- and post-reading and listening vocabulary tasks
- Glossing of receptive vocabulary
- Recycling throughout each part and online

MODERATELY SCAFFOLDED

Guided exercises focus on comprehension, application, and clarification of productive skills.

VOCABULARY STRATEGIES

Vocabulary strategy sections focus on form, use, and meaning to help students process complex content.

TRANSITION LEVEL

CEFR B2+–C1 **GSE** 68–80

A deep dive for transition-level students, the Transition level mirrors the academic rigor of college courses.

INTENSIVE SKILL PRACTICE

Intensive skill practice tied to learning objectives informed by the Global Scale of English

AUTHENTIC CONTENT

- Readings: 200–3,500-words
- Lectures: 25 minutes

CONTENT AND FLUENCY VOCABULARY APPROACH

- No direct vocabulary instruction
- Online vocabulary practice for remediation

Key Features

A consistent and systematic format in every chapter enables students to build confidence as they master essential fundamental and critical thinking skills.

CHAPTER STRUCTURE

CHAPTER PROFILE
This overview establishes context with visuals to provide interest and schema-building.

OUTCOMES
Sequenced, recycled, and carefully integrated, outcomes focus on developing language skills and are informed by Pearson's Global Scale of English.

GETTING STARTED
An engaging, visual-based task activates learner schema and motivates students to engage with the content.

LISTEN
A variety of thematically-related listenings highlight key concepts. These are accompanied by skill presentation, critical thinking, collaboration, and practical application tasks.

SPEAK
Theme-related tasks with careful step-by-step instruction tied to learner outcomes prepare students to integrate content, grammar, and vocabulary as they move through the stages of the speaking process.

GRAMMAR FOR SPEAKING
Dedicated grammar presentation and practices prepare students for authentic speaking tasks.

BUILDING VOCABULARY
A targeted approach to vocabulary instruction with practical, high-frequency lexical sets gives students tools to expand their vocabulary.

APPLY YOUR SKILLS
Extensive practical application allows students to practice the skills developed in the chapter.

DEVELOP SOFT SKILLS
Task-based strategies focus on college readiness, social and cultural awareness, and academic study.

Students are engaged from the first page, with unit openers that feature high-interest images related to the chapter themes. Chapter openers include a stimulating content-based image and an overview of the chapter's topics and skills.

A **video introduction** at the beginning of each unit gives students an academic perspective.

A **chapter profile** outlines the chapter content to prepare students for the listening and speaking they will do in the chapter.

Outcomes aligned with the Global Scale of English are clearly stated to ensure student awareness of skills.

Chapter 1   Building the World We Live In

CHAPTER PROFILE

Architecture is the style and design of buildings and spaces. Architects plan buildings where people live, study, work, and play. They also design outdoor spaces, like parks.

This chapter is about places where people live, and ways architects help make them better.

You will listen to

· a lecture about artificial islands.

· a presentation about vertical gardens.

You will also

· role-play a conversation about living spaces.

· ask and answer questions about your living space.

· take a class survey about classmates' living spaces.

OUTCOMES

· Predict before you listen

· Ask and answer simple questions

· Form questions with *wh*-words

· Identify and use compound nouns

· Learn about how university students find places to live

For more about ARCHITECTURE, see Chapter 2. See also RW ARCHITECTURE, Chapters 1 and 2.

2   UNIT 1   ARCHITECTURE

Engaging and high-interest listenings allow students to connect with the academic content as they develop fundamental comprehension and critical thinking skills.

GETTING STARTED

Look at these photos and the photo on page 2. Answer these questions with a partner.

1. Which photo shows the following?
   - an island made by people
   - a garden on a building
   - a building in a small space

2. Why do you think architects built these places? Match these reasons to the pictures.
   - to make clean air
   - to save space in the city
   - to make places for people to live
   - to make a place more beautiful
   - to grow food

3. Do you know where these places are?

Go to MyEnglishLab to complete a self-assessment.

LISTEN

SKILL: PREDICTING

When you **predict**, you think about what you are going to hear about the topic.

Before you listen, think about the

- **speaker(s):** Who is speaking? A teacher? A classmate? A friend? A family member?
- **situation:** Where is the speaker? In a classroom? At home? What is happening? Is the speaker teaching you something? Is it a friendly conversation?
- **topic:** What is the speaker talking about?

Then predict what you will hear.

- **words and phrases:** What words or phrases do you think you will hear about the topic?

Building the World We Live In   3

GETTING STARTED sections use visuals to build schema.

LISTEN sections provide structured presentation and practice of key listening skills.

Skill presentations provide clear explanations and examples.

Vocabulary and **previewing** exercises support the unique needs of beginning students as they work to build the necessary language skills that will enable them to manage challenging academic lectures in the future.

VOCABULARY PREVIEW

A. Read the sentences. Look at the boldfaced words. Do you know what they mean? Share your ideas with a partner.

1. Don't drink the water. It is **dirty**.
2. People need **air** to live.
3. Living space is a big **problem** in cities like Tokyo and New York.
4. My mother has many **plants** and flowers in her garden.
5. That house is big. It takes up a lot of **space**.
6. The **side** of that house is blue.
7. Trees need sun and water to **grow**.
8. I like that park. It has **beautiful** flowers and trees.

Exercises blend **gist- and detail-focused tasks** to help students develop extensive and intensive listening skills and top-down and bottom-up comprehension strategies.

C. Listen to the excerpts from the lecture. Read the sentences. Circle *T* (true) or *F* (false). Correct the false statements.

SECTION 1

T / F   1. Air pollution, or dirty air, is a big problem in big cities.

_____

T / F   2. There are many green spaces in big cities.

_____

SECTION 2

T / F   3. Trees, plants, and flowers help make the air clean.

_____

T / F   4. Trees make oxygen which we need to live.

_____

T / F   5. A vertical garden grows on the ground.

_____

T / F   6. Vertical gardens need a lot of space.

_____

SECTION 3

T / F   7. Not many cities are making vertical gardens.

_____

T / F   8. The vertical gardens are only in the United States.

Good speaking skills are an essential component of communication. Developing speaking skills is necessary for students to succeed both inside and outside the classroom and to ensure their success in future careers. Speaking skills studied include asking and answering simple questions, expressing likes and dislikes, describing people and places, giving instructions for a process, comparing and contrasting, stating opinions, and expressing agreement and disagreement.

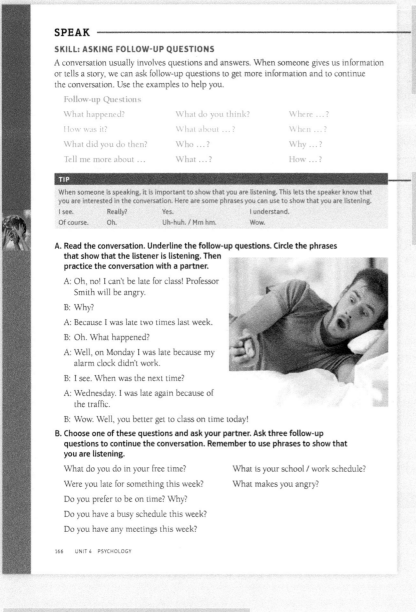

SPEAK sections provide clear presentations to help language learners focus on the skills they need to become successful speakers.

Tips throughout the chapter include helpful information and scaffolding to support beginning language learners.

Remember boxes allow students to demonstrate understanding of the skill.

REMEMBER

Think about how you predict. Complete the sentences.

Before you listen, think about the _____ , _____ , and _____ .

Then predict the _____ and _____ that you will hear.

Students are introduced to the speaking process with step-by-step speaking instructions. There is extensive use of graphic organizers throughout the process.

ROLE-PLAY A CONVERSATION ABOUT LIVING SPACES

STEP 1: LISTEN BEFORE YOU SPEAK

A. Look at the photo. Think about the speakers, the situation, and the topic. Then predict the words or phrases you will hear. Complete the chart.

Speakers	
Situation	
Topic	
Words and Phrases	

Step 1 scaffolds the task with prediction and vocabulary previewing.

STEP 2: PREPARE TO SPEAK

A. Read the conversation. Underline all of the questions. Then practice the conversation with a partner. Take turns reading Alberto's and Ava's parts.

Alberto:	Hello! I know you! You are in my class.
Ava:	Oh, hi! I'm Ava. Yes, we are in English class together. What is your name?
Alberto:	I'm Alberto. Nice to see you again. How do you know about this coffee shop? It is far from our school.
Ava:	I live in an apartment near here.
Alberto:	I see. Do you like it?
Ava:	Yes. I like it a lot. There's a large living space, and it has a garden. Where do you live?

Step 2 provides a model conversation and prepares students for the speaking task.

STEP 3: SPEAK

Practice your conversation with your partner. Then role-play your conversation in front of the class. Follow these tips:

• Look at your partner when you speak. (Make eye contact.)

• Try to break the sentences into smaller parts. Look up as you read each small part.

• Smile and speak naturally.

In **Step 3**, students integrate content, speaking skills, grammar, and vocabulary as they move through the speaking process.

STEP 4: PEER FEEDBACK

Listen to your classmates' role plays. Choose two pairs to give feedback to. Write the students' names, the questions they ask, and the new vocabulary words they use. Check (✓) *Yes* or *No* for eye contact.

Step 4 guides students through a peer review and discussion to expand their speaking skills.

Students' Names	Questions and Vocabulary Words	Eye Contact
		☐ Yes ☐ No
		☐ Yes ☐ No

Dedicated grammar presentation and practice prepare students for authentic writing tasks. Tasks focus on form, use, and meaning and move from controlled to practical application.

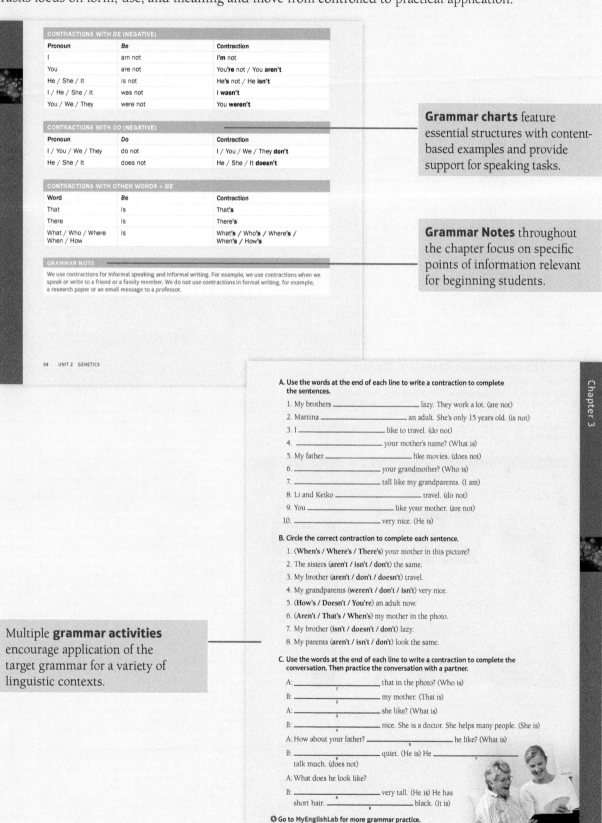

Grammar charts feature essential structures with content-based examples and provide support for speaking tasks.

Grammar Notes throughout the chapter focus on specific points of information relevant for beginning students.

Multiple **grammar activities** encourage application of the target grammar for a variety of linguistic contexts.

CONTRACTIONS WITH BE (NEGATIVE)

Pronoun	Be	Contraction
I	am not	I'm not
You	are not	You're not / You aren't
He / She / It	is not	He's not / He isn't
I / He / She / It	was not	I wasn't
You / We / They	were not	You weren't

CONTRACTIONS WITH DO (NEGATIVE)

Pronoun	Do	Contraction
I / You / We / They	do not	I / You / We / They don't
He / She / It	does not	He / She / It doesn't

CONTRACTIONS WITH OTHER WORDS + BE

Word	Be	Contraction
That	is	That's
There	is	There's
What / Who / Where / When / How	is	What's / Who's / Where's / When's / How's

GRAMMAR NOTE

We use contractions for informal speaking and informal writing. For example, we use contractions when we speak or write to a friend or a family member. We do not use contractions in formal writing, for example, a research paper or an email message to a professor.

58   UNIT 2   GENETICS

Chapter 3

A. Use the words at the end of each line to write a contraction to complete the sentences.

1. My brothers _____ lazy. They work a lot. (are not)
2. Martina _____ an adult. She's only 15 years old. (is not)
3. I _____ like to travel. (do not)
4. _____ your mother's name? (What is)
5. My father _____ like movies. (does not)
6. _____ your grandmother? (Who is)
7. _____ tall like my grandparents. (I am)
8. Li and Keiko _____ travel. (do not)
9. You _____ like your mother. (are not)
10. _____ very nice. (He is)

B. Circle the correct contraction to complete each sentence.

1. (**When's / Where's / There's**) your mother in this picture?
2. The sisters (**aren't / isn't / don't**) the same.
3. My brother (**aren't / don't / doesn't**) travel.
4. My grandparents (**weren't / don't / isn't**) very nice.
5. (**How's / Doesn't / You're**) an adult now.
6. (**Aren't / That's / When's**) my mother in the photo.
7. My brother (**isn't / doesn't / don't**) lazy.
8. My parents (**aren't / isn't / don't**) look the same.

C. Use the words at the end of each line to write a contraction to complete the conversation. Then practice the conversation with a partner.

A: _____ that in the photo? (Who is)
B: _____ my mother. (That is)
A: _____ she like? (What is)
B: _____ nice. She is a doctor. She helps many people. (She is)
A: How about your father? _____ he like? (What is)
B: _____ quiet. (He is) He _____ talk much. (does not)
A: What does he look like?
B: _____ very tall. (He is) He has short hair. _____ black. (It is)

🔵 Go to MyEnglishLab for more grammar practice.

We Are   59

A mix of academic and high-frequency vocabulary provides the fundamental building blocks with which students can construct comprehension and meaningful speech.

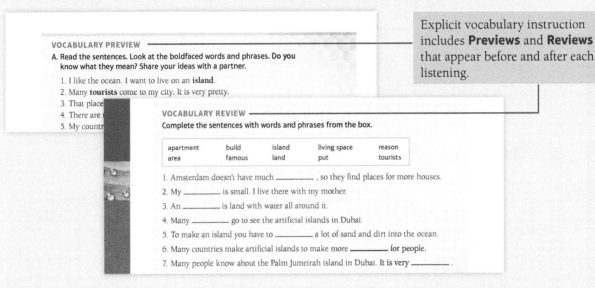

VOCABULARY PREVIEW

A. Read the sentences. Look at the boldfaced words and phrases. Do you know what they mean? Share your ideas with a partner.

1. I like the ocean. I want to live on an **island**.
2. Many **tourists** come to my city. It is very pretty.
3. That place
4. There are
5. My countr

VOCABULARY REVIEW

Complete the sentences with words and phrases from the box.

apartment	build	island	living space	reason
area	famous	land	put	tourists

1. Amsterdam doesn't have much _____ , so they find places for more houses.
2. My _____ is small. I live there with my mother.
3. An _____ is land with water all around it.
4. Many _____ go to see the artificial islands in Dubai.
5. To make an island you have to _____ a lot of sand and dirt into the ocean.
6. Many countries make artificial islands to make more _____ for people.
7. Many people know about the Palm Jumeirah island in Dubai. It is very _____ .

Explicit vocabulary instruction includes **Previews** and **Reviews** that appear before and after each listening.

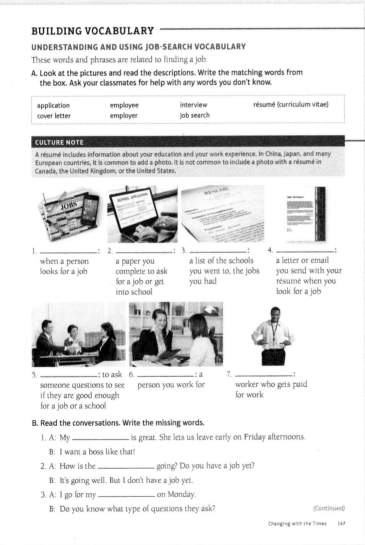

BUILDING VOCABULARY

UNDERSTANDING AND USING JOB-SEARCH VOCABULARY

These words and phrases are related to finding a job.

A. Look at the pictures and read the descriptions. Write the matching words from the box. Ask your classmates for help with any words you don't know.

application	employee	interview	résumé (curriculum vitae)
cover letter	employer	job search	

CULTURE NOTE

A résumé includes information about your education and your work experience. In China, Japan, and many European countries, it is common to add a photo. It is not common to include a photo with a résumé in Canada, the United Kingdom, or the United States.

1. _____ : when a person looks for a job
2. _____ : a paper you complete to ask for a job or get into school
3. _____ : a list of the schools you went to, the jobs you had
4. _____ : a letter or email you send with your résumé when you look for a job

5. _____ : to ask someone questions to see if they are good enough for a job or a school
6. _____ : a person you work for
7. _____ : worker who gets paid for work

B. Read the conversations. Write the missing words.

1. A: My _____ is great. She lets us leave early on Friday afternoons.
   B: I want a boss like that!
2. A: How is the _____ going? Do you have a job yet?
   B: It's going well. But I don't have a job yet.
3. A: I go for my _____ on Monday.
   B: Do you know what type of questions they ask?

(Continued)

BUILDING VOCABULARY sections help students understand new words and phrases related to the themes. Engaging practice activities follow the presentation.

Culture Notes aid comprehension and expand understanding of a broad range of cultural topics.

Each chapter concludes with an Apply Your Skills section that includes practical applications. The section can also function as an assessment.

APPLY YOUR SKILLS

In this chapter, you listened to a podcast about different ideas of time. You did a role play about finding a good roommate. In Apply Your Skills, you will listen to a discussion about how different cultures think about time. Then you will have a group discussion about your opinions of time.

The **introduction** provides a recap of the chapter so far and a preview of what is to come.

PREDICT

Look at the pictures. Think about the speaker, the situation, and the topic. Then predict the words and phrases you will hear. Complete the chart.

Speaker	
Situation	
Topic	
Words and Phrases	

Predict activities activate students' background knowledge about the topic and context of the listening.

Think Visually provides an opportunity for students to analyze charts, graphs, photos, and other visuals.

THINK VISUALLY

There are different time zones in the world. On a map, the starting point for time zones is Greenwich, England. This is called Greenwich Mean Time (GMT).

For cities around the world, we write time zones with the number of hours difference from GMT and "+" (later) or "–" (earlier).

For example,
+ 2 = GMT + 2 hours, or two hours later than GMT.
– 5 = GMT – 5 hours, or five hours earlier than GMT.

Students apply new vocabulary and structures from the chapter to complete a practical, communicative **assignment** such as a class survey, a presentation, or a guided group discussion.

ASSIGNMENT

Write questions for a class survey about living spaces. Ask your classmates the questions and report on the survey.

Strategies for academic success, life skills, and career readiness skills—such as using graphic organizers, communicating with instructors, and giving peer feedback—appear in each chapter. These soft skills help increase students' confidence and ability to cope with challenges of academic study and college culture.

DEVELOP SOFT SKILLS

UNDERSTANDING CULTURAL ATTITUDES ABOUT PERSONAL SPACE

Every country has a unique culture. Culture is the history, beliefs, and traditions of a place, and the attitudes and behaviors of the people who grow up there. Understanding different cultural attitudes is an important part of communication and relationships.

Glossary

imagine: form pictures and ideas in your mind
touching: putting your hand on something or someone
hug: put your arms around someone and hold him or her to show love or friendship
whisper: speak very quietly into someone's ear
aware: If you are aware of something, you know it is happening.

A **glossary** features challenging vocabulary items essential for understanding the text.

A. Look at the pictures. Who are the people? What is their relationship? Write your ideas. Then compare with a partner.

Visuals, including photos and realia, complement the article, supporting understanding and enhancing interest.

A: How do you study for an exam?

B: I study with a classmate. I sometimes cram the night before the exam. How about you?

A: I study at home. I review my notes.

2. How do you usually feel before / during / after an exam? Complete the sentences with adjectives from the box, or use your own ideas. Then tell a partner.

I feel _____ before an exam.

I feel _____ during an exam.

I feel _____ after an exam.

Comprehension practice is followed by **personalized reflection** on the soft skill.

At the end of each chapter, students complete a **skill self-assessment checklist**.

WHAT DID YOU LEARN?

Check (✓) the skills and vocabulary you learned. Circle the things you need to practice.

SKILLS

☐ I can listen for reasons.
☐ I can ask follow-up questions.
☐ I can use *because* and *because of* with reasons.
☐ I can tell time.
☐ I can understand cultural attitudes about personal space.

VOCABULARY

☐ angry	☐ exercise	☐ midnight	☐ relationship
☐ at a time	☐ fixed	☐ most	☐ rely on
☐ club	☐ flexible	☐ noon	☐ schedule
☐ comfortable	☐ follow	☐ on time	☐ several
☐ culture	☐ half past	☐ organize	☐ situation
☐ end	☐ it depends	☐ personal	
☐ excited	☐ meeting	☐ prefer	

A BLENDED APPROACH

University Success integrates a tailored online lab populated with engaging multimedia content including videos, slide presentations, and audio, which can be used for presenting new content and skills, as well as practice and extension activities for students to complete in class or as homework. All MyEnglishLab activities are referenced throughout the Student Books.

MyEnglishLab includes an easy-to-use online management system that offers a flexible gradebook and tools for monitoring student success.

TEACHER RESOURCES

Downloadable step-by-step teaching notes for each chapter offer suggestions and a "library" of teaching tips for teaching skills and content

Essential tools such as audio scripts, answer keys, and course planners help in lesson planning

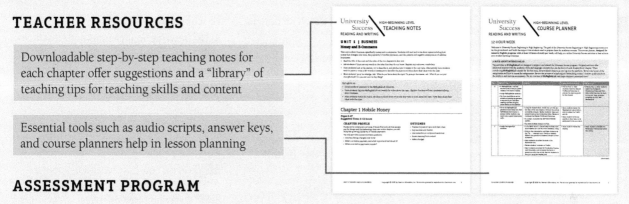

ASSESSMENT PROGRAM

University Success has several different types of assessments that provide opportunities for teachers to gauge learning. These assessments can be used as pre-course diagnostics, chapter achievement tests, mid-course assessments, and final summative assessments. The flexible nature of these assessments allows teachers to choose which assessments will be most appropriate at various stages of the program. These assessments are available in MyEnglishLab in both Word and PDF formats. There are formative assessments embedded in the Student Book.

HOW WOULD YOU LIKE TO ASSESS YOUR STUDENTS?

Assessment	Where to Find	How to Use
Skill Self-Assessments	MyEnglishLab	• At the beginning and end of every chapter for students to identify skill areas for improvement • To provide data that can inform lesson planning
Achievement Tests	MyEnglishLab	• As a summative assessment at the end of each chapter
Apply Your Skills	Student Book	• As a diagnostic assessment to inform students' strengths and weaknesses before they complete a chapter • As a formative assessment, in which students complete this section or parts of this section after they complete the chapter
Mid-Term Exam	MyEnglishLab	• As a summative assessment at the end of Units 1 and 2
Final Exam	MyEnglsihLab	• As a summative assessment at the end of Units 3 and 4
Writing / Speaking Skill Assessment	Student Book	• Writing and Speaking Tasks: As formative assessments to evaluate practical application of skills presented
Vocabulary Quiz	Student Book	• *Vocabulary Previews / Reviews:* As a diagnostic to inform teaching and lesson planning • As formative assessments to assess student understanding of vocabulary
Grammar Quiz	Student Book	• *Grammar tasks:* As a diagnostic to identify student understanding of grammar points • As formative assessments to assess student understanding of grammar points
Skill, Vocabulary, Grammar Assessments	MyEnglishLab	• Any activity in MyEnglishLab to be used as formative assessments to assess student understanding of chapter-related content

Scope and Sequence

	LISTENING SKILLS	SPEAKING SKILLS

Unit 1 Architecture
STRUCTURAL SCIENCE

Chapter 1 Building the World We Live In

LISTENINGS
- A lecture about artificial islands
- A conversation about living spaces
- A presentation about vertical gardens

Predict	Ask and Answer Simple Questions **TASK** Role-play a conversation about living spaces **TASK** Take a class survey about living spaces

Chapter 2 Interesting Places and Spaces

LISTENINGS
- A presentation about hotels around the world
- A conversation about a school campus and classrooms
- A lecture about a new kind of classroom

Listen for details	Describe places **TASK** Describe your campus and classroom **TASK** Describe ideas for changing your classroom

Unit 2 Genetics
NATURAL SCIENCE

Chapter 3 Who We Are

LISTENINGS
- A podcast about genetics and personality
- People describing their roommates
- A class discussion about how hobbies connect to genetics

Listen for gist	Describe people **TASK** Give a short presentation about a roommate **TASK** Describe three relatives

Chapter 4 How We Learn

LISTENINGS
- A lecture about genetics and learning
- Short presentations about learning styles
- A discussion about genetics and language learning

Listen for examples	Express degrees of like and dislike **TASK** Give a short presentation about your learning style **TASK** Suggest language learning activities

Unit 3 Business and Technology
BUSINESS

Chapter 5 In-store or Online

LISTENINGS
- A panel discussion about in-store and online shopping
- People comparing stores and websites
- A lecture about how e-commerce ideas can help local stores

Understand words and phrases for comparing and contrasting	State an opinion / Express agreement and disagreement **TASK** Give a short presentation comparing two stores or websites and their products **TASK** Give a presentation about products

Chapter 6 Changing with the Times

LISTENINGS
- A sales presentation about 3-D printing
- A talk about how to start a business
- A presentation about how to find a job

Listen for instructions and steps	Ask for and give instructions **TASK** Give instructions for an activity or a process **TASK** Give instructions for a skill

Unit 4 Psychology
HUMANITIES

Chapter 7 On Time

LISTENINGS
- A podcast about different ideas of time
- Conversations about finding a roommate
- A discussion about time in different cultures

Listen for reasons	Ask follow-up questions **TASK** Role-play a conversation about finding a roommate **TASK** Have a group discussion about your opinions of time

Chapter 8 The Habit Cycle

LISTENINGS
- A podcast about how we can start and stop a habit
- A conversation about helping a friend do better in school
- A talk about habits of successful people

Ask for clarification and repetition	Make and respond to suggestions **TASK** Give suggestions to classmates for changing their habits **TASK** Give a presentation about how you spend and manage your time

GRAMMAR SKILLS	BUILDING VOCABULARY	SOFT SKILLS	MYENGLISHLAB
			Video: An Introduction about Architecture
Form questions with *Wh*-words	Identify and use compound nouns	Find a place to live TASK Compare living spaces on and off campus	Skill self-assessments Online practice: • listening • grammar • vocabulary
Understand and use prepositions of location	Understand and use reaction expressions	Find people, places, and things on campus TASK Talk about common places on a college campus	Skill self-assessments Online practice: • listening • grammar • vocabulary Challenge listening: **Madrid's Vertical Gardens**
			Video: An Introduction about Genetics
Understand and use contractions	Understand and use antonyms	Learn how to give great presentations TASK Give a presentation about a famous person	Skill self-assessments Online practice: • listening • grammar • vocabulary
Use *like* + infinitive verb forms	Identify and use collocations	Know your personal learning style TASK Compare your learning style with a classmate's	Skill self-assessments Online practice: • listening • grammar • vocabulary Challenge listening: **Genetics and Academics**
			Video: An Introduction about Business and Technology
Understand and use comparative adjectives	Understand and use large numbers	Stay safe online TASK Make a list of tips for staying safe online	Skill self-assessments Online practice: • listening • grammar • vocabulary
Understand and use imperatives	Understand and use job-search vocabulary	Use graphic organizers to study vocabulary TASK Create a graphic organizer for studying vocabulary	Skill self-assessments Online practice: • listening • grammar • vocabulary Challenge listening: **Social Media and Business**
			Video: An Introduction about Psychology
Use *because* and *because of* with reasons	Tell time	Understand cultural attitudes about personal space TASK Talk about personal space in your culture	Skill self-assessments Online practice: • listening • grammar • vocabulary
Use *should / shouldn't* for suggestions	Recognize and use *-ed* adjectives	Study for exams TASK Give suggestions for studying for an exam	Skill self-assessments Online practice: • listening • grammar • vocabulary Challenge listening: **The Coffee Habit**

Acknowledgments

I am grateful for everyone's hand in *University Success*—from the beginning visionary stages to the final edits. Many thanks to Amy McCormick for bringing me on to this project and Debbie Sistino for keeping us on track. Special thanks to my dear colleague and friend, Jaimie Scanlon, for her help with direction and ideas. It was a wonderful collaborative project that I was happy to be a part of. Thank you.

—*Cynthia Fettig*

Reviewers

We would like to thank the following reviewers for their many helpful comments and suggestions:

Jamila Barton, North Seattle Community College, Seattle, WA; **Joan Chamberlin**, Iowa State University, Ames IA; **Lyam Christopher**, Palm Beach State College, Boynton Beach, FL; **Robin Corcos**, University of California, Santa Barbara, Goleta, CA; **Tanya Davis**, University of California, San Diego, CA; **Brendan DeCoster**, University of Oregon, Eugene, OR; **Thomas Dougherty**, University of St. Mary of the Lake, Mundelein, IL; **Bina Dugan**, Bergen County Community College, Hackensack, NJ; **Bonnie Duhart**, Lone Star College, University Park, TX; **Priscilla Faucette**, University of Hawaii at Manoa, Honolulu, HI; **Lisa Fischer**, St. Louis University, St. Louis, MO; **Kathleen Flynn**, Glendale Community College, Glendale, CA; **Mary Gawienowski**, William Rainey Harper College, Palatine, IL; **Sally Gearhart**, Santa Rosa Junior College, Santa Rosa, CA; **Carl Guerriere**, Capital Community College, Hartford, CT; **Vera Guillen**, Eastfield College, Mesquite, TX; **Angela Hakim**, St. Louis University, St. Louis, MO; **Pamela Hartmann**, Evans Community Adult School, Los Angeles Unified School District, Los Angeles, CA; **Shelly Hedstrom**, Palm Beach State University, Lake Worth, FL; **Sherie Henderson**, University of Oregon, Eugene, OR; **Lisse Hildebrandt**, English Language Program, Virginia Commonwealth University, Richmond, VA; **Barbara Inerfeld**, Rutgers University, Piscataway, NJ; **Bessie Karras-Lazaris**, California State University, Northridge, CA; **Zaimah Khan**, Northern Virginia Community College, Loudon Campus, Sterling, VA; **Tricia Kinman**, St. Louis University, St. Louis, MO; **Kathleen Klaiber**, Genesee Community College, Batavia, NY; **Kevin Lamkins**, Capital Community College, Hartford, CT; **Noga Laor**, Long Island University, Brooklyn, NY; **Mayetta Lee**, Palm Beach State College, Lake Worth, FL; **Kirsten Lillegard**, English Language Institute, Divine Word College, Epworth, IA; **Craig Machado**, Norwalk Community College, Norwalk, CT; **Cheryl Madrid**, Spring International Language Center, Denver, CO; **Ann Meechai**, St. Louis University, St. Louis, MO; **Melissa Mendelson**, Department of Linguistics, University of Utah, Salt Lake City, UT; **Tamara Milbourn**, University of Colorado, Boulder, CO; **Debbie Ockey**, Fresno City College, Fresno, CA; **Diana Pascoe-Chavez**, St. Louis University, St. Louis, MO; **Raymond Purdy**, ELS Language Centers, Princeton, NJ; **Kathleen Reynolds**, William Rainey Harper College, Palatine, IL; **Linda Roth**, Vanderbilt University ELC, Greensboro, NC; **Minati Roychoudhuri**, Capital Community College, Hartford, CT; **Bruce Rubin**, California State University, Fullerton, CA; **Margo Sampson**, Syracuse University, Syracuse, NY; **Elena Sapp**, Oregon State University, Corvallis, OR; **Sarah Saxer**, Howard Community College, Ellicott City, MD; **Anne-Marie Schlender**, Austin Community College, Austin, TX; **Susan Shields**, Santa Barbara Community College, Santa Barbara, CA; **Barbara Smith-Palinkas**, Hillsborough Community College, Dale Mabry Campus, Tampa, FL; **Sara Stapleton**, North Seattle Community College, Seattle, WA; **Lisa Stelle**, Northern Virginia Community College Loudon, Sterling, VA; **Jamie Tanzman**, Northern Kentucky University, Highland Heights, KY; **Ariana Van Beurden**, Oregon State University, Corvallis, OR; **Jeffrey Welliver**, Soka University of America, Aliso Viejo, CA; **Mark Wolfersberger**, Brigham Young University, Hawaii, Laie, HI; **May Youn**, California State University, Fullerton, CA

Architecture

➤ Go to **MyEnglishLab** to see an introduction about **ARCHITECTURE**.

Chapter 1   Building the World We Live In

CHAPTER PROFILE

Architecture is the style and design of buildings and spaces. Architects plan buildings where people live, study, work, and play. They also design outdoor spaces, like parks.

This chapter is about places where people live, and ways architects help make them better.

You will listen to

• a lecture about artificial islands.

• a presentation about vertical gardens.

You will also

• role-play a conversation about living spaces.

• ask and answer questions about your living space.

• take a class survey about classmates' living spaces.

OUTCOMES

• Predict before you listen

• Ask and answer simple questions

• Form questions with *wh*-words

• Identify and use compound nouns

• Learn about how university students find places to live

For more about **ARCHITECTURE**, see Chapter 2. See also [RW] **ARCHITECTURE**, Chapters 1 and 2.

GETTING STARTED

Look at these photos and the photo on page 2. Answer these questions with a partner.

1. Which photo shows the following?
   - an island made by people
   - a garden on a building
   - a building in a small space

2. Why do you think architects built these places? Match these reasons to the pictures.
   - to make clean air
   - to save space in the city
   - to make places for people to live
   - to make a place more beautiful
   - to grow food

3. Do you know where these places are?

🔾 Go to **MyEnglishLab** to complete a self-assessment.

LISTEN

SKILL: PREDICTING

When you **predict**, you think about what you are going to hear about the topic.

Before you listen, think about the

- **speaker(s):** Who is speaking? A teacher? A classmate? A friend? A family member?

- **situation:** Where is the speaker? In a classroom? At home?
  What is happening? Is the speaker teaching you something? Is it a friendly conversation?

- **topic:** What is the speaker talking about?

Then predict what you will hear.

- **words and phrases:** What words or phrases do you think you will hear about the topic?

For each photo, think about the speaker, the situation, and the topic. Then predict the words and phrases you will hear. Complete the charts.

1	Speaker	
	Situation	
	Topic	
	Words and Phrases	

2	Speaker	
	Situation	
	Topic	
	Words and Phrases	

Sun energy

3	Speakers	
	Situation	
	Topic	
	Words and Phrases	

REMEMBER

Think about how you predict. Complete the sentences.

Before you listen, think about the _____ , _____ , and _____ .
Then predict the _____ and _____ that you will hear.

CULTURE NOTE

People in different cultures show that they are listening in different ways. Some people nod their heads up and down when they are listening. Some people make a sound. Others close their eyes or look down. Some people ask questions or add to the conversation. How do you show you are listening?

VOCABULARY PREVIEW

A. Read the sentences. Look at the boldfaced words and phrases. Do you know what they mean? Share your ideas with a partner.

1. I like the ocean. I want to live on an **island**.
2. Many **tourists** come to my city. It is very pretty.
3. That place is very **famous**. Many people go there.
4. There are many **reasons** to build an island.
5. My country is very small. It does not have much **land**.
6. The country **put** a lot of houses on that island.
7. We need more **living space**. There are not a lot of houses for all the people.
8. In the city, most people live in **apartments**.
9. I go to that **area** often. It is a nice place.
10. John knows how to **build** houses.

B. Write the boldfaced words and phrases from Part A next to their definitions.

_____ 1. places where people live with bedrooms, a living room, a kitchen

_____ 2. land with water all around it

_____ 3. people who travel to visit a place

_____ 4. put pieces together to make something

_____ 5. known by many people; popular

_____ 6. an area where people live

_____ 7. a part of a place

_____ 8. why something happens

_____ 9. a piece of ground that people own

_____ 10. placed or moved something

C. You will hear these sentences in the listening. Read them aloud with a partner. Do you remember the meanings of the boldfaced words and phrases?

1. This is an artificial **island** in Dubai.
2. Many countries make islands for **tourists** to visit.
3. Other countries also have **famous** artificial islands.
4. What are some other **reasons** for making an island?
5. Some countries are small and do not have much **land**.
6. The Japanese made an island next to Osaka. They **put** a large airport there.
7. Other countries use islands to make more **living space**.
8. In Amsterdam, they needed more houses and **apartments.**
9. There was an **area** with many rocks in the ocean near San Francisco.
10. One last reason to **build** an artificial island is for energy.

⊙ Go to **MyEnglishLab** to complete a vocabulary practice.

PREDICT

Look at the photo. Think about the speaker, the situation, and the topic.
Then predict the words or phrases you will hear. Complete the chart.
Then share your ideas with a partner.

Speaker	
Situation	
Topic	
Words and Phrases	

LISTEN

A. Listen. Check (✓) if your predictions are correct or incorrect. For any that are incorrect, write the correct information.

	Correct	Incorrect	Correct Information
Speaker			
Situation			
Topic			
Words and Phrases			

B. Check (✓) the main idea of the lecture.

☐ 1. artificial islands for tourists

☐ 2. reasons people build artificial islands

☐ 3. living space in big cities

☐ 4. artificial islands in Canada

C. Listen to the excerpts from the lecture. Circle the correct word or phrase.

SECTION 1

1. The speaker is talking about a(n) (**famous park / artificial island / apartment**) in Dubai.

2. It is the shape of a(n) (**island / flower / tree**).

3. Some countries build islands that are (**interesting / living spaces / dangerous**) for tourists.

SECTION 2

4. Some small countries build islands to have more (**people / land / airplanes**).

5. In Osaka, there was no land for an (**airport / apartment building / park**).

SECTION 3

6. Some countries want to make more (**people / living space / islands**).

7. The city of Amsterdam made six islands for (**tourists / houses / cars**).

8. The city of Montreal put (**dirt / trains / rocks**) in a river to make an island.

9. In an area of San Francisco, it was dangerous for (**people / ships / trains**).

10. Many countries build islands to make (**land / houses / energy**) from the wind or sun.

LISTEN AGAIN

A. Listen again. Read the sentences. Circle *T* (true) or *F* (false). Correct the false statements. Use the example to help you.

T /(F) 1. Dubai does not have any artificial islands.

_____Dubai has artificial islands._____

T / F 2. Some countries make artificial islands for tourists.

_____.

T / F 3. Osaka has an artificial island for houses.

_____.

T / F 4. Some countries make artificial islands to add more living space.

_____.

T / F 5. Amsterdam made three islands to add houses for 30,000 people.

_____.

T / F 6. It is easy to make an artificial island in deep water.

_____.

T / F 7. Many countries build islands to make energy.

_____.

B. Complete the chart with the information about each island.

Island Name	Where It Is	Reason to Build	Other Information
Palm Jumeirah			
IJburg			
Notre Dame			
Treasure Island			

C. Circle your opinion. Then practice the conversation with your partner. Take turns with A and B roles.

A: What do you think about artificial islands?

B: I think they are (**good / bad**).

A: Why?

B: I think they are good because (**people need more land for houses / tourists come / they make the area safe**).

OR

B: I think they are bad because (**they are not real / too many tourists come / they cost a lot of money**).

VOCABULARY REVIEW

Complete the sentences with words and phrases from the box.

apartment	build	island	living space	reason
area	famous	land	put	tourists

1. Amsterdam doesn't have much _____ , so they find places for more houses.

2. My _____ is small. I live there with my mother.

3. An _____ is land with water all around it.

4. Many _____ go to see the artificial islands in Dubai.

5. To make an island you have to _____ a lot of sand and dirt into the ocean.

6. Many countries make artificial islands to make more _____ for people.

7. Many people know about the Palm Jumeirah island in Dubai. It is very _____ .

8. One _____ people make an artificial island is to make a place for tourists.

9. The _____ around San Francisco was not safe for ships.

10. It is not easy to _____ an artificial island in the ocean.

Go to **MyEnglishLab** for more listening practice.

SPEAK

SKILL: ASKING SIMPLE QUESTIONS

People ask questions to get more information. When we ask a question, it also shows that we are interested in the conversation.

Questions often start with

- *What* (What is that?)

- *Where* (Where do you live?)

- *Who* (Who do you live with?)

- *How* (How do you get to school?)

A. Read the conversation. Underline the questions. Then practice the conversation with a partner.

A: Where do you live?

B: I live near the university.

A: Who do you live with?

B: I live with my parents.

A: How do you get to school?

B: I take the bus.

B. Write a question to complete the conversations. Then practice the conversations with a partner. Take turns with A and B roles.

1. A: _____?

   B: I study at the coffee shop.

2. A: _____?

   B: I live with my parents.

3. A: _____?

   B: I drive my car.

4. A: _____?

   B: My birthday is in April.

5. A: _____?

   B: Because I have a test tomorrow.

6. A: _____?

   B: I have three brothers.

REMEMBER

Read the questions. Then write the correct answer from the box.

What Where Why Who How When	ask questions	to get more information

1. Why do people ask questions?

   _____

2. Which words can you use to start a question?

   _____

3. How can you show you are interested in a conversation?

   _____

These charts show how to form questions in the present form.

QUESTIONS WITH *BE*		
Question Word	***Be* (*am* / *is* / *are*)**	**Subject**
Where	is	your building?
Who	are	the other students there?
How big	is	your room?

QUESTIONS WITH *DO* / *DOES*				
Question Word	**Auxiliary Verb (*Do* / *Does*)**	**Subject**	**Verb**	
Where	do	they	live?	
Why	does	he	live	far away?
How	do	they	get	to school?

Look at the chart for how to form *wh*-questions with *be* and *do*.

WH-QUESTIONS WITH *BE* AND *DO* / *DOES*					
Who **What** **Where** **When** **Why** **How**	am	I	...?	**Who** **What** **Where** **When** **Why** **How**	**do**	I you we they	...?
	is	he she it	...?				
	are	we you they	...?		**does**	he she it	...?

A. Complete the questions with *do, does, is,* or *are.*

1. Where _____ she live?

2. Why _____ the rooms so small?

3. What _____ the reasons to build an island?

4. How far away _____ your school?

5. What _____ the famous islands in Dubai?

6. How big _____ your room?

7. Why _____ the people live on the island?

8. How _____ he get home from work?

B. Write the words in the correct order to make a question.

1. do / people / why / make / islands?

   _____?

2. your family / live / does / where

   _____?

3. is / in your apartment / what

   _____?

4. the islands / are / how big

   _____?

5. you / where / do / live

   _____?

6. lives / on / who / island / that

   _____?

7. are / the islands / where

   _____?

8. the island / how long / is

   _____?

C. Write a question to complete each conversation.

1. A: _____?

   B: I live in an apartment.

2. A: _____?

   B: Tourists come to the island because they like the beach.

3. A: _____?

   B: Countries build islands to make more living space.

4. A: _____?

   B: They take sand from the ocean to build an island.

5. A: _____?

   B: The famous artificial island in Dubai is Palm Jumeirah.

6. A: _____?

   B: Treasure Island is near San Francisco.

7. A: _____?

   B: The islands in Amsterdam are used for houses.

8. A _____?

   B: The island is 4.83 kilometers (3 miles) long.

↻ **Go to MyEnglishLab for more grammar practice.**

ROLE-PLAY A CONVERSATION ABOUT LIVING SPACES

STEP 1: LISTEN BEFORE YOU SPEAK

A. Look at the photo. Think about the speakers, the situation, and the topic. Then predict the words or phrases you will hear. Complete the chart.

Speakers	
Situation	
Topic	
Words and Phrases	

B. Read the words and their meanings. You will hear these words in the conversation.

> **Glossary**
>
> far: a long distance; not near
> large: big, wide
> garden: land used to grow plants, flowers, or vegetables
> parents: mother, father
> hard: difficult; not easy
> loud: making a lot of noise
> roommate: a person you share a room with; not a family member

C. Listen to the conversation. Complete the chart.

	Ava	Alberto
Where do they live?		
Describe their living spaces.		
Where do they study?		

D. Match the answers to the questions. Write the correct letter next to each question.

_____ 1. How do the people know each other?

_____ 2. Where is the coffee shop?

_____ 3. Where does Ava live?

_____ 4. Where does Alberto live?

_____ 5. Why is it hard for Alberto to study at home?

_____ 6. Where does Ava study?

_____ 7. Where does Alberto study?

a. It is far from their school.

b. His brothers are loud.

c. They know each other from English class.

d. He lives with his family.

e. She studies at the library.

f. He studies at the coffee shop.

g. She lives in an apartment near the coffee shop.

STEP 2: PREPARE TO SPEAK

A. Read the conversation. Underline all of the questions. Then practice the conversation with a partner. Take turns reading Alberto's and Ava's parts.

Alberto:	Hello! I know you! You are in my class.
Ava:	Oh, hi! I'm Ava. Yes, we are in English class together. What is your name?
Alberto:	I'm Alberto. Nice to see you again. How do you know about this coffee shop? It is far from our school.
Ava:	I live in an apartment near here.
Alberto:	I see. Do you like it?
Ava:	Yes. I like it a lot. There's a large living space, and it has a garden. Where do you live?
Alberto:	I live in my parents' house.
Ava:	Do you like living with your family?
Alberto:	I like it, but sometimes it is hard to study.
Ava:	Why is it hard to study?
Alberto:	My little brothers are loud.
Ava:	Oh, I understand. My roommate is loud, too. I study at the library. Where do you study?
Alberto:	I study at this coffee shop. It's quiet, and the coffee is good!

B. You will work with a partner to write your own conversation about living spaces. Use the chart to plan your ideas.

Who are the people?	
Where does each person live?	
What do they like about their living spaces?	
What do they dislike (not like)?	
What questions do they ask?	

C. Write your conversation on a separate sheet of paper. Give each speaker five lines. Use *wh*-questions and new vocabulary from this chapter.

STEP 3: SPEAK

Practice your conversation with your partner. Then role-play your conversation in front of the class. Follow these tips:

- Look at your partner when you speak. (Make eye contact.)
- Try to break the sentences into smaller parts. Look up as you read each small part.
- Smile and speak naturally.

STEP 4: PEER FEEDBACK

Listen to your classmates' role plays. Choose two pairs to give feedback to. Write the students' names, the questions they ask, and the new vocabulary words they use. Check (✓) *Yes* or *No* for eye contact.

Students' Names	Questions and Vocabulary Words	Eye Contact
		☐ Yes ☐ No
		☐ Yes ☐ No

BUILDING VOCABULARY

IDENTIFYING AND USING COMPOUND WORDS

Sometimes we put two or more words together to make one word. These are called **compound words**.

A. Read these examples of compound words with a partner. What two words make each one?

apartment building	bedroom	coffee shop	student housing
bathroom	bus stop	roommate	train station

B. Read the sentences. Look at the boldfaced compound words. Do you know what they mean? Share your ideas with a partner.

1. How many people live in that new **apartment building**?

2. Do you have a **roommate**, or do you live alone?

3. All new students must live in **student housing**.

4. I can't sleep. My **bedroom** is on the first floor. It's noisy.

5. How many **bathrooms** does your house have?

6. My house is near the **train station**.

7. There is a new **coffee shop** in my town.

8. I walk to the **bus stop** every morning.

C. Write five questions to ask a partner. Use a different compound noun from Part A in each one.

1. _____

2. _____

3. _____

4. _____

5. _____

○ Go to **MyEnglishLab** to complete a vocabulary practice.

APPLY YOUR SKILLS

In this chapter, you listened to a lecture about why people build artificial islands. You wrote and practiced a conversation about living spaces. In Apply Your Skills, you will listen about a way people are making better living spaces. You will ask your classmates questions about where they live.

VOCABULARY PREVIEW

A. **Read the sentences. Look at the boldfaced words. Do you know what they mean? Share your ideas with a partner.**

1. Don't drink the water. It is **dirty**.

2. People need **air** to live.

3. Living space is a big **problem** in cities like Tokyo and New York.

4. My mother has many **plants** and flowers in her garden.

5. That house is big. It takes up a lot of **space**.

6. The **side** of that house is blue.

7. Trees need sun and water to **grow**.

8. I like that park. It has **beautiful** flowers and trees.

B. **Write the boldfaced words from Part A next to their definitions.**

_____ 1. trees, flowers, and other green living things

_____ 2. a part of something that is not the front, back, top, or bottom

_____ 3. something that is difficult

_____ 4. an area that is empty, available to use

_____ 5. not clean

_____ 6. the gas all around us; we need this to live

_____ 7. get bigger in size

_____ 8. pretty

⊙ Go to **MyEnglishLab** to complete a vocabulary practice.

PREDICT

Look at the photos. Think about the speaker, the situation, and the topic.
Then predict the words or phrases that you will hear. Complete the chart.

Speaker	
Situation	
Topic	
Words and Phrases	

Vertical Gardens = Clean Cities

LISTEN

🎧 A. Listen to the lecture. Were your predictions correct? Which ones? Tell a partner.

My prediction was correct / incorrect about …

B. Check (✓) the main idea of the lecture.

☐ 1. Big cities have dirty air.
☐ 2. There are no trees, plants, or flowers in big cities.
☐ 3. Vertical gardens can help clean the air in big cities.
☐ 4. A vertical garden grows on the side of a building.

🎧 C. Listen to the excerpts from the lecture. Read the sentences. Circle *T* (true) or *F* (false). Correct the false statements.

SECTION 1

T / F   1. Air pollution, or dirty air, is a big problem in big cities.

_____

T / F   2. There are many green spaces in big cities.

_____

SECTION 2

T / F   3. Trees, plants, and flowers help make the air clean.

_____

T / F   4. Trees make oxygen which we need to live.

_____

T / F   5. A vertical garden grows on the ground.

_____

T / F   6. Vertical gardens need a lot of space.

_____

SECTION 3

T / F   7. Not many cities are making vertical gardens.

_____

T / F   8. The vertical gardens are only in the United States.

_____

LISTEN AGAIN

A. Listen again. Complete the sentences with words and phrases from the box.

| beautiful | buses | clean | dirty air | trains | trucks |
| buildings | cars | dirty | flowers | trees | |

1. A big city has a lot of _____, _____, _____, _____, _____ and _____.

2. A big city doesn't have many _____ or _____.

3. Trees and plants can _____ dirty air.

4. Vertical gardens are good because they are _____ and they help clean the _____ air.

B. Work with a partner. Discuss the questions.

1. How do trees and plants help us?

2. How are vertical gardens good for a city? How are artificial islands good for a city?

3. What do you think of vertical gardens?

C. Write two questions about vertical gardens. Use wh-words (Who, What, Where, When, Why, How long / big) about vertical gardens. Ask your questions to the class.

_____

_____

VOCABULARY REVIEW

Complete the sentences with words from the box.

| air | dirty | plants | side | beautiful | grow | problem | space |

1. Big cities often have _____ air.
2. Vertical gardens grow on the _____ of a building.
3. What kinds of flowers and _____ are in your garden?
4. Vertical gardens make the _____ clean.
5. Pollution, or dirty air, is a big _____ for cities around the world.
6. There is a _____ garden on the side of that building.
7. Vertical gardens _____ on buildings.
8. Gardens take a lot of _____ on the ground.

THINK VISUALLY

A. Look at the diagram of a vertical garden. Answer the questions.

1. Where does the dirt go?
   a. into the water bottle
   b. into the cup
   c. on top of the plant

2. Where is the plant?
   a. at the bottom
   b. at the top
   c. under the dirt

3. How does the plant get water?
   a. comes up from the water bottle
   b. from the top
   c. from the side

4. How many steps are there to make this vertical garden?
   a. four
   b. five
   c. six

How to Make an Indoor Vertical Garden

plant

dirt

cup

4
3
2
1

B. Think of another way to design a vertical garden.
Draw a simple diagram. Then share your drawing with a partner.

GRAMMAR

FORMING *WH*-QUESTIONS

Use the words to write a *wh*-question.

1. is / vertical garden / what / a

_____?

2. do / people / why / gardens / plant

_____?

3. trees / plants / do / how / and / the air / clean / make

_____?

4. grow / a / where / vertical garden / does

_____?

5. are / some / big problems / what / the city / in

_____?

6. does / the air / get dirty / how / in / the city

_____?

ASSIGNMENT

Write questions for a class survey about living spaces. Ask your classmates the questions and report on the survey.

PREPARE TO SPEAK

A. Think of questions to ask your classmates. Think of three questions. Use vocabulary and grammar from the chapter.

You can ask questions about

- their living space

- the city they live in

- problems in their city

B. Write your questions.

1. _____

2. _____

3. _____

C. Share your questions with a partner. Check each other's questions. Correct any mistakes.

SPEAK

A. Walk around the class and ask your questions to three classmates. Write each classmate's name and answers.

	Classmates' Names	Answers to Your Questions
1.		Question 1: Question 2: Question 3:
2.		Question 1: Question 2: Question 3:
3.		Question 1: Question 2: Question 3:

B. Work in a group. Take turns sharing your questions and your classmates' answers.

⬆ Go to **MyEnglishLab** to complete grammar and vocabulary practices.

DEVELOP SOFT SKILLS

FINDING A PLACE TO LIVE

Many students move to a new place for university. Some students live on campus (at the university). But that is not the only choice. Some students live off campus. They may live with their families or they can get their own place to live. There are many things to think about when you choose where to live.

A. Listen to the presentation. Answer the questions.

> **Glossary**
>
> rent: pay money to live in a house or apartment
>
> fee: money paid to use something
>
> cafeteria: a type of restaurant, usually in an office or school, where people get food

On-campus housing—a dormitory room

Off-campus housing—a bedroom in an apartment

1. Rooms on campus don't have _____ .
   a. furniture
   b. a kitchen
   c. electricity

2. It is good to live on campus because _____ .
   a. it's easy to make friends
   b. you may need to buy furniture
   c. apartments are big

3. If you want an apartment off campus, look for one _____ .
   a. in your neighborhood
   b. far from the university
   c. near a bus stop

4. When you rent an apartment, you usually pay _____ .
   a. the same
   b. less
   c. more

B. Listen to the conversation. Discuss the questions with your classmates.

1. Why do you think Junseo lives far away?

2. How far away do you live from campus?

3. How long does it take you to get to class?

C. Do you live on campus or off campus? Talk with a partner about where you live. Say one thing you like and one thing you don't like about where you live.

WHAT DID YOU LEARN?

Check (✓) the skills and vocabulary you learned. Circle the things you need to practice.

SKILLS

☐ I can predict before I listen.   ☐ I can identify and use compound nouns.

☐ I can ask and answer simple questions.   ☐ I can find a place to live.

☐ I can form questions with *wh*-words.

VOCABULARY

☐ air	☐ dirty	☐ problem
☐ apartment	☐ famous	☐ put
☐ area	☐ ground	☐ reason
☐ beautiful	☐ island	☐ side
☐ breathe	☐ land	☐ space
☐ build	☐ living space	☐ tourists
☐ clean	☐ plant	

● Go to **MyEnglishLab** to complete a self-assessment.

Chapter 2 | Interesting Places and Spaces

CHAPTER PROFILE

Architects build many kinds of places. They design apartment buildings, shopping centers, schools, hotels, and more. Sometimes the places they build are very interesting or unusual. This chapter is about interesting places and the objects inside them.

You will listen to

• a presentation about hotels around the world.

• a conversation about a school campus and classrooms.

• a lecture about a new kind of classroom.

You will also

• describe your campus and classroom.

• describe ideas for changing your classroom.

OUTCOMES

• Listen for details

• Describe places

• Understand and use prepositions of location

• Understand and use reaction expressions

• Find people, places, and things on campus

For more about **ARCHITECTURE**, see Chapter 1. See also [RW] **ARCHITECTURE**, Chapters 1 and 2.

GETTING STARTED

Work with a partner. Look at these photos and the photo on page 24. What is interesting or unusual about these places?

◐ Go to **MyEnglishLab** to complete a self-assessment.

LISTEN

SKILL: LISTENING FOR DETAILS

In Chapter 1, you listened for the main idea. When you listen for **details**, you listen for specific information that helps you know more about a topic. You often need to listen for **details**.

Details may be

- names
- numbers
- dates
- times
- places
- reasons
- examples
- instructions

To listen for **details**

- think about your reasons for listening.
- think about your own questions about the topic.
- ask yourself
  - What do I need to know?
  - What questions do I have?
  - What type of details am I listening for?

Question Words	Types of Details
Who ...?	a person, a name
When ...?	a day, date, year, or time
How ...?	instructions, a description
What is ...?	an example
Where ...?	a place
What happened ...?	an event
Why ...?	a reason or explanation
How many ...?	a number

A. Read the words and phrases in the box. What types of details do you need to listen for? Complete the chart below. Use the words and phrases from the box to write a question for each answer.

| How do you … ? | How many … ? | What is … ? | Where is … ? | Why do … ? |
| How long … ? | How tall … ? | When … ? | Who is … ? | |

	Questions	Answers
1.		The Bluebird is a hotel in a tree.
2.		The rooms have two beds.
3.		The hotel will open in April.
4.		The architect is George Winslow.
5.		The bed is 2 meters (6 feet) long.
6.		The hotel has 30 floors.
7.		The Hôtel Monet is in Paris.
8.		I like to stay there because it's interesting.
9.		To go to your room, you take the elevator.

B. Work with a partner. Read the situation. Talk about the types of details you need to listen for. Complete the chart.

SITUATION

You are in class. Your teacher is talking about the homework assignment. What type of details do you need to listen for?

	Question	Listen for …
1.	What is the assignment?	
2.	How many pages?	
3.	When is the assignment due?	

C. Listen to the teacher. Answer the questions to complete the notes.

1. What is the assignment?	Write about _____.
	Describe _____.
	Explain _____.
2. How many pages?	_____ pages
3. When is the assignment due?	Due on _____.

D. Read the situation. Preview the discussion questions on the class handout.

SITUATION

You are in class. Your teacher is giving a lecture about the architecture of hotels around the world. The class will discuss these questions after the lecture

Lecture: Hotel Architecture around the World

Discussion questions

1. Where is the hotel?
2. Who is the architect?
3. When did they build the hotel?
4. Why is the hotel famous?
5. How many swimming pools does the hotel have?
6. What do the windows look like?

E. Work with a partner. For each discussion question in Part D, think about the type of details you need to listen for. Write the types of details from the box next to questions on the handout.

| date | name (of a person) | place (city or country) |
| description | number | reason or explanation |

F. Preview the questions. Think about the types of details you need to listen for. Then listen to the lecture and write the answers.

Discussion Questions	Your Answers
1. Where is the hotel?	
2. Who is the architect?	
3. When did they build the hotel?	
4. Why is the hotel famous?	
5. How many swimming pools does the hotel have?	
6. What do the windows look like?	

REMEMBER

Complete the missing information about how to listen for details.

1. Think about your _____ for listening.
2. _____
   before you listen. Or think about your own questions about the topic.
3. Ask yourself, _____
   _____ .

VOCABULARY PREVIEW

A. Read the sentences. Look at the boldfaced words and phrases. Choose the sentence with the same meaning. Compare your answers with a partner.

1. Jian's apartment building is very **tall**. It has 80 floors.
   a. Jian's apartment building is very big.
   b. Jian's apartment building is very small.

2. That hotel has a **normal** bed and a bathroom.
   a. That hotel room is not special.
   b. That hotel room is special and different.

3. Rebecca and David **stay** at beautiful hotels. They take a lot of vacations.
   a. Rebecca and David work at beautiful hotels.
   b. Rebecca and David sleep at beautiful hotels.

4. You will have a great **experience** at the Bluebird Hotel.
   a. You will enjoy your time at the Bluebird Hotel.
   b. You will pay a lot of money at the Bluebird Hotel.

5. That hotel is very **interesting**. It does not look like other hotels.
   a. The hotel is different.
   b. The hotel is boring.

6. Henri goes to that hotel **every** month.
   a. Henri goes to that hotel during all the months.
   b. Henri goes to that hotel only a few months.

7. Mohammed reads a lot of books about old architecture. It is his **hobby**.
   a. Mohammed doesn't like architecture.
   b. Mohammed likes architecture very much.

8. Marisa and Tom **love** that restaurant. They eat there often.
   a. Marisa and Tom don't like the food at that restaurant.
   b. Marisa and Tom like the food at that restaurant.

9. Junko likes **nature**. She walks in the forest every Saturday.
   a. Junko likes trees, plants, and being outside.
   b. Junko likes to plant gardens.

10. We **suggest** the treehouse hotel in Costa Rica. It is very beautiful.
    a. We like it and want others to go there.
    b. We do not want others to go there.

11. Our **trip** to Egypt was fun.
    a. They lived in Egypt.
    b. They traveled to Egypt.

B. You will hear these sentences in the listening. Complete the sentences with the boldfaced words from Part A.

1. A hotel is a _____ building with many rooms.

2. A _____ hotel room does not have much in it.

3. Some tourists _____ at a hotel for a new _____ .

4. Architects build hotels in some very _____ places.

5. Architects build hotels for _____ interest and _____ .

6. This hotel is for people who _____ airplanes.

7. People who love _____ and trees stay at the Bellavista.

8. Do you want to stay at an interesting hotel? Then I _____ taking a _____ to Giraffe Manor in Kenya.

⏺ Go to **MyEnglishLab** to complete a vocabulary practice.

Interesting Places and Spaces   29

PREDICT

A. Look at the pictures. Think about the speaker, the situation, and the topic.
Then predict the words and phrases you will hear. Complete the chart.

Interesting Hotels
Around the World

Speaker	
Situation	
Topic	
Words and Phrases	

B. Preview the questions about the presentation. Check (✓) the type of detail you need to listen for to answer each question.

Questions	Types of Details to Listen For			
1. Why do people stay in interesting hotels?	☐ Place	☐ Description	☐ Date	☐ Reason
2. Where is the Jumbo Stay Hotel?	☐ Name	☐ Place	☐ Reason	☐ Date
3. Who designed the Bellavista hotel in Costa Rica?	☐ Name	☐ Number	☐ Place	☐ Description
4. What kind of hotel is the Manta Resort?	☐ Place	☐ Description	☐ Date	☐ Reason
5. How many books are in the library hotel?	☐ Name	☐ Place	☐ Number	☐ Date
6. What kind of people stay at the V8 Hotel?	☐ Number	☐ Description	☐ Date	☐ Reason
7. What hotel does the speaker suggest?	☐ Name	☐ Place	☐ Date	☐ Reason
8. When did architects build the Giraffe Manor?	☐ Number	☐ Date	☐ Reason	☐ Description
9. Why does the Giraffe Manor have tall windows?	☐ Place	☐ Description	☐ Date	☐ Reason
10. Why is dinner an interesting experience?	☐ Name	☐ Place	☐ Reason	☐ Date

LISTEN

A. Listen to the presentation. Check (✓) the main idea.

☐ 1. Interesting hotels cost a lot of money.

☐ 2. There are many interesting hotels around the world.

☐ 3. Interesting people stay at interesting hotels.

B. Listen to the excerpts from the presentation. Circle the correct details.

SECTION 1

1. People stay in interesting hotels because they (**want to have a new experience / do not have a lot of money**).

SECTION 2

2. The Jumbo Stay Hotel is in (**the rainforest / Sweden / a library**).

3. A (**brother and sister / father and daughter / husband and wife**) made a hotel in the rainforest.

4. The Manta Resort is a hotel under the (**park / ocean / street**).

5. The Library Hotel has (**hundreds / thousands / millions**) of books.

6. People who love (**nature / cars / trees**) stay at the V8 Hotel.

SECTION 3

7. The speaker suggests the (**V8 Hotel / Giraffe Manor / Library Hotel**).

8. The Giraffe Manor is in (**Germany / the rainforest / Kenya**).

9. Architects finished the hotel in (**1903 / 1930 / 1913**).

10. The hotel has tall windows because (**it is old / giraffes come inside / it is in the trees**).

11. Dinner is interesting because people (**see / eat / study**) giraffes in the restaurant.

LISTEN AGAIN

🔊 A. Listen to the presentation again. Complete the chart with notes about each hotel.

Hotel	City / Country	Details
Jumbo Stay		
Bellavista		
Manta Resort		
Library Hotel		
V8 Hotel		
Giraffe Manor		

B. Complete the conversation with your own ideas. Then practice the conversation with three classmates. Take turns with A and B roles.

A: Which hotel do you want to stay in?

B: I want to stay in the _____ hotel.

A: Why?

B: Because I like / love / want to _____ .

VOCABULARY REVIEW

Complete the sentences with words and phrases from the box.

experiences	interesting	nature	stay	tall	every
hobby	love	normal	suggest	trip	

1. In Costa Rica, there is a hotel in the rainforest. You can sleep in the _____ trees!

2. On my next _____ to New York City, I want to go to the Library Hotel.

3. This hotel is very big. _____ floor has 100 rooms.

4. People who love _____ and animals go to the Giraffe Manor in Kenya.

5. I _____ giraffes! They are my favorite animal.

6. My family loves to travel. We have many fun _____ together.

7. I love the ocean. Can you _____ a hotel near the water?

8. I think _____ hotels are boring. I like to visit a special place.

9. In the summer, we _____ at a hotel at the ocean.

10. Sven's _____ is cars. He knows about many kinds of cars.

11. There are so many _____ hotels in the world. They are all so different from normal hotels. I want to stay at every one!

⬆ Go to **MyEnglishLab** for more listening practice.

SPEAK

SKILL: DESCRIBING PLACES

When you describe a place, you give details about it. You explain what is there and describe the objects in the place. Here are some useful phrases and vocabulary to describe places.

Useful Phrases	Examples	
There is / There are *There aren't any*	**There is** a garden. **There are** many flowers.	
has / have *does not have a / any*	The hotel **has** many books. The rooms **have** tall windows. It **does not have** a swimming pool.	
It is (not) + adjective Noun + *be* + adjective	**It is** near. **It is not** far. The hotel **is** beautiful. The rooms **are** big.	The island **is** famous. The place **is not** interesting. The building **is** tall. The hotel **is not** normal.

🔊 A. Look at the pictures. Listen. Which place does the person describe? Circle *a* or *b*.

1. a

   b

2. a

   b

B. Work with a partner. Take turns describing the pictures in Part A. Try to guess the picture. Use the example to help you.

A: The room is small. It does not have any windows.

B: Is it this picture?

A: Yes / No. _____

REMEMBER

Complete the missing information.

When you describe a place, you give _____ about it. You tell what is there, and you describe the _____ in the place.

Some useful phrases to describe places are:

_____

_____

Some adjectives to describe places are:

_____

_____

Grammar for Speaking — Understanding and using prepositions of location

Prepositions of location describe an object's location. They describe where the object is. Prepositions of location are useful when you describe places.

Prepositions	Examples		Prepositions	Examples	
in		The students are **in** the classroom.	below / under		The blackboard is **below** / **under** the clock.
on		The clock is **on** the wall.	above / over		The clock is **above** / **over** the desk.
next to		The tree is **next to** the school.	in front of		The tree is **in front of** the student center.
between		The tree is **between** two hotels.	in back of / behind		The tree is **in back of** / **behind** the school.

A. Look at the pictures. Complete the sentences with prepositions from the box.

above	between	in front of	on
behind	in	next to	under

1. The teacher is _____ the desk.

2. There are pictures _____ the wall.

3. There is a plant _____ the desk.

4. There are three students _____ the class.

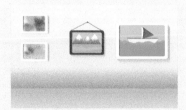

5. There is a garden _____ the building.

6. There is a light _____ the table.

7. There are books _____ the chair.

8. The classroom is _____ the office and the music room.

B. Look around your classroom. Write five sentences about the room. Use phrases for describing places and prepositions of location.

1. _____

2. _____

3. _____

4. _____

5. _____

🔊 Go to **MyEnglishLab** for more grammar practice.

DESCRIBE YOUR CAMPUS OR CLASSROOM

STEP 1: LISTEN BEFORE YOU SPEAK

A. Look at the photo. Think about the speaker, the situation, and the topic. Then predict the words and phrases you will hear. Complete the chart.

Speaker	
Situation	
Topic	
Words and Phrases	

B. Review the words and definitions. You will hear these words in the conversation.

Glossary

great: very good

gym: large room with machines for exercise

wonderful: very good

dormitory: large room or building where a lot of people sleep

convenient: useful and easy

short: not tall

cool: interesting

C. Listen to the conversation. Complete the chart with words and phrases from the box.

chairs	computers	dormitory	gardens
coffee shops	desks	video screen	gym

Objects on the Campus	Objects in the Classroom

D. Listen again. Read the sentences. Circle *T* (true) or *F* (false). Correct the false statements.

T / F 1. The campus does not have any coffee shops.

_____

T / F 2. Jessica's dormitory is next to the gym.

_____

T / F 3. There are gardens behind every building.

_____

T / F 4. The classes are between the restaurants and the gym.

_____

T / F   5. There are special desks in the classroom.

_____

T / F   6. Every desk has a computer.

_____

T / F   7. The classroom has a video screen.

_____

STEP 2: PREPARE TO SPEAK

A. Work with a partner. Practice the conversation. Then plan a conversation about your campus or classroom.

Junko: Hello?

Jessica: Hi Junko. It's Jessica.

Junko: Oh, Hi Jessica! How are your classes going?

Jessica: They're going well! I really like my school.

Junko: That's great! What do you like about it?

Jessica: Well, the campus is very beautiful, and it has everything.

Junko: Like what?

Jessica: It has a lot of restaurants and coffee shops. The gym is wonderful, and it is next to my dormitory. And there are beautiful gardens in front of every building.

Junko: Where are your classrooms?

Jessica: They are in between the restaurants and the gym. It's very convenient.

Junko: How are the classrooms?

Jessica: Really nice! Every desk can either be tall or short. You can sit or stand.

Junko: That's interesting. Are there computers on the desks?

Jessica: There are a few computers in the front of the room. But there aren't any computers on the desks. There is a large video screen on the wall.

Junko: How cool!

Jessica: Yes, I love it here! I suggest this school to everyone!

B. Work with your partner. Plan your conversation. List things on your campus and in your classroom. Complete the chart.

Things on My Campus	Things in My Classrooms

C. Use the conversation in Part A. Write a new conversation. Describe your campus and your classroom. Use the examples to help you.

My campus is beautiful / big / small / modern.

My classroom has tables / desks / large windows.

There is / There are / There aren't any …

It has / They have / It doesn't have any …

The _____ is in / on / next to / between / behind / in front of …

STEP 3: SPEAK

A. Practice your conversation with a partner. Take turns with A and B roles.

1. Look at each other when you speak.

2. Speak naturally.

3. Smile.

Conversation:

A: Hi _____ ! How are your classes going?

B: They are going well! I really like my school.

A: Great! What do you like about it?

B. Join one or two other pairs. Take turns performing your conversations.

STEP 4: PEER FEEDBACK

Give feedback to your group members. Write the students' names in the chart. Listen to the conversation. Write details about the campus or classroom they describe. Then complete the feedback checklist.

Students' names:	
Campus	Classroom
Feedback checklist	
The conversation …	The speakers …
☐ described a campus and a classroom.	☐ looked at each other.
☐ used phrases for describing places (*It has / There is / There are*, etc.).	☐ smiled.
☐ used prepositions of location (*in / on / in front of*, etc.).	

BUILDING VOCABULARY

EXPRESSING REACTIONS WITH ADJECTIVES

In a conversation, there are many ways to react (respond) to what someone says. Here are some useful expressions.

	☺		☹	
That's …	great.	beautiful.	terrible.	too bad.
How …	wonderful.	interesting.	sad.	awful.
	cool.	nice.		

A. Complete the conversations with a reaction expression from the chart above. Then practice the conversations with a partner.

1. A: I love my campus.

   B: _____ .

2. A: How do you like your school?

   B: It's very old. I don't like it.

   A: _____ .

3. A: How are the classrooms at your school?

   B: They're very modern and they have new computers.

   A: _____ .

4. A: How is your dormitory?

   B: It's a very tall building. There are many stairs, but it doesn't have an elevator.

   A: _____ .

B. Work with a partner. Read the question. Then complete the conversation with an answer and a reaction expression.

1. A: Do you like your classes?

   B: _____ .

   A: _____ . (reaction)

2. A: Is your campus convenient?

   B: _____ .

   A: _____ . (reaction)

3. A: What do you love about your campus or classroom?

   B: I love the _____ .

   A: _____ . (reaction)

❂ Go to **MyEnglishLab** to complete a vocabulary practice.

APPLY YOUR SKILLS

In this chapter, you listened to a lecture about interesting hotels around the world. You listened to people describe a campus and a classroom. You described your campus and classroom. In Apply Your Skills, you will listen to a lecture about new architecture and design for classrooms. You will think of an idea to help students learn in the classroom.

VOCABULARY PREVIEW

A. Read the sentences. Look at the boldfaced words. Do you know what they mean? Share your ideas with a partner.

1. I study **better** when it is quiet.

2. I want to **change** my room. I want the bed next to the window.

3. Walking to class is a **healthy** way to get to school.

4. Don't sit at your desk too long. You need to get up and **move**.

5. The teacher wants us to **focus** on our homework.

6. My brother has a lot of **energy**. He runs everywhere he goes.

7. My classmates **agree** with me. We think the test was too difficult.

8. What **percent** of students like their classes?

B. Write the boldfaced words from Part A next to their definitions.

_____ 1. make something different

_____ 2. a feeling of not being tired

_____ 3. change position, be active

_____ 4. think well and clearly

_____ 5. have the same opinion or idea

_____ 6. strong and well in your body

_____ 7. more than good

_____ 8. %, an amount out of every one hundred

◐ Go to **MyEnglishLab** to complete a vocabulary practice.

PREDICT

Look at the pictures. Think about the speaker, the situation, and the topic. Then predict the words and phrases you will hear. Complete the chart.

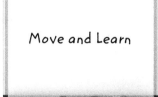

Move and Learn

Speaker	
Situation	
Topic	
Words and Phrases	

LISTEN

A. Listen to the lecture. Were your predictions correct? Which ones? Tell a partner. Use the example to help you.

My prediction was correct / incorrect about …

B. Circle the ideas the teacher talks about.

large balls to sit on	chairs that move	pictures on the wall
a slide instead of stairs	big tables	desks that move up or down

C. Listen to the excerpts from the lecture. Read the sentences. Circle *T* (true) or *F* (false). Correct the false statements.

SECTION 1

T / F   1. The students' classroom has tall desks to stand at.

_____

T / F   2. When we move, we think better.

_____

SECTION 2

T / F   3. A school in Taiwan has a slide instead of stairs.

_____

T / F   4. Students study better when they sit for eight hours every day.

_____

(Continued)

T / F   5. Students like classrooms where they can move.

_____

T / F   6. The teacher wants the students to sit down.

_____

LISTEN AGAIN

🎧 Listen again. Circle the best word to complete the answer. Then practice the conversations with a partner.

1. A: How can we learn better?
   B: We can learn better when we (**move / sit**).

2. A: What helps some students learn?
   B: A (**tall chair / large ball**) can help some students learn.

3. A: How long do students sit every day?
   B: Most students sit (**five / eight**) to nine hours a day.

4. A: What percent do students like school more because their chairs move?
   B: (**74 / 72 / 84**) percent of students like school more.

VOCABULARY REVIEW

Complete the sentences with words from the box.

agree	change	focus	move
better	energy	healthy	percent

1. It is not _____ to sit all day in a chair.

2. It's important for students to _____ their bodies during the school day.

3. Architects and classroom designers are helping to make schools _____ .

4. Scientists _____ that chairs that can move are good for students.

5. Eighty-four _____ of students think school is more interesting when their chairs move.

6. Scientists suggest that schools _____ their classrooms and use chairs that move.

7. Students have a lot of _____ . It is important for them to move.

8. The large balls in this classroom help students _____ more on their work.

THINK VISUALLY

**A. Listen. What do students say about their experiences with chairs that move?
Write these phrases under the correct bar on the graph.**

| like school better | get better grades | think class is more interesting |

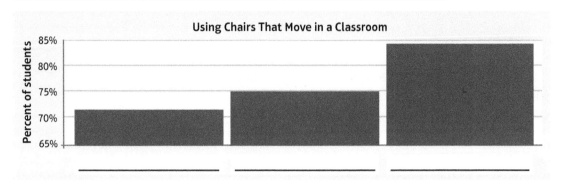

Using Chairs That Move in a Classroom

_____   _____   _____

B. Work with a partner. Take turns asking and answering these questions.

1. How many students say they like school better because of the chairs that move?

2. How many students say they get better grades because of the chairs that move?

3. How many students say class is interesting because of the chairs that move?

GRAMMAR

USING PREPOSITIONS OF LOCATION

**A. Work with a partner. Look at the maps of the campus and the classroom. Ask
and answer the questions. Use phrases for describing places and prepositions
of location.**

Classroom

1. Where is the teacher's desk?

2. Where is the window?

3. Where is the door?

4. Where is the clock?

5. Where are the computers?

6. Where is the plant?

Campus

1. Where is the gym?

2. Where is the restaurant?

3. Where is the coffee shop?

4. Where is the garden?

5. Where is the dormitory?

6. Where are the classrooms?

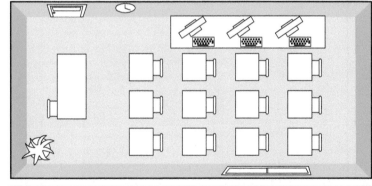

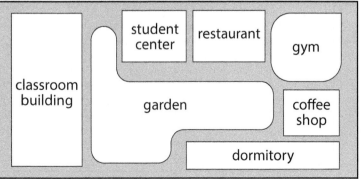

B. Work with a partner. Ask and answer three questions about the things in your classroom.

ASSIGNMENT

Think of ways to change your classroom to help students learn better. Present your ideas to the class.

PREPARE TO SPEAK

A. Think of ways to change the classroom to help students learn better. Write your ideas in the chart. Use the examples to help you.

Move the desks in the classroom.

Put students' work on the wall.

Put flowers on every desk.

	Ideas
1.	
2.	
3.	
4.	

B. Draw a picture of your classroom with the changes.

SPEAK

A. Describe your classroom to the class. Show your picture. Use the preposition of location in the box and the example phrases.

above	in	in back of	in front of	on	under

My classroom has …

The students have …

There is / are …

It doesn't have any …

B. Listen to your classmates' ideas. Choose three and take notes. Write each classmate's name in the chart. Write details about their ideas.

Classmates' Names	Details

🔾 Go to **MyEnglishLab** to complete grammar and vocabulary practices.

DEVELOP SOFT SKILLS

FINDING PEOPLE, PLACES, AND THINGS ON CAMPUS

Do you know your way around campus? Your time at university will be very busy. Learn your way around early! Walk around your campus. See what is out there. What you find may surprise you. A university is more than just offices and classrooms. There are also fun things to see and do!

Glossary

arts and humanities building: a place where students can learn about subjects like art, history, and languages

athletics complex: where you go to exercise or do indoor sports, like swimming, or basketball

dining hall: a place to buy and eat food

health center: a place to receive medical advice

registrar: where the university keeps important documents

science building: a place where students can learn about subjects like physics, biology, and chemistry

student center: a place to meet other students

A. Work with a partner or in a group. Discuss the questions.

1. Read the list of places on a university campus. Which ones are on your campus?

2. What happens at each place?

3. Which places do you go to?

arts and humanities building	dormitories (dorms)	registrar
athletics complex	health center	science building
dining hall	library	student center

B. Listen to a conversation between two students, Honza and Marta. Marta is helping Honza find places on campus. Write the three places he is going to.

1. _____

2. _____

3. _____

C. Listen again. Read the statements. Circle *T* (true) or *F* (false). Correct the false statements.

T / F   1. Marta and Honza are at the dormitory now.

_____

T / F   2. The registrar is between the coffee shop and the supermarket.

_____

T / F   3. The health center is on Regent Avenue.

_____

T / F   4. The student center is in front of the health center.

_____

T / F   5. The student center has a dining hall, a movie theater, and a gym.

_____

D. Write three places or buildings on a university campus. Then write two activities you can do at each place.

student center—meet friends, watch a movie

E. Work with a partner. Say the activities, but don't name the place. Can your partner guess the building?

WHAT DID YOU LEARN?

Check (✓) the skills and vocabulary you learned. Circle the things you need to practice.

SKILLS

☐ I can listen for details.

☐ I can describe places.

☐ I can understand and use prepositions of location.

☐ I can understand and use reaction expressions.

☐ I can find people, places, and things on campus.

VOCABULARY

☐ agree

☐ better

☐ change

☐ energy

☐ every

☐ experience

☐ focus

☐ healthy

☐ hobby

☐ interesting

☐ love

☐ move

☐ nature

☐ normal

☐ percent

☐ stay

☐ suggest

☐ tall

☐ trip

⊙ Go to **MyEnglishLab** to complete a self-assessment.

⊙ Go to **MyEnglishLab** for a challenge listening about Architecture.

Genetics

Go to **MyEnglishLab** to to see an introduction about **GENETICS**.

Chapter 3   Who We Are

CHAPTER PROFILE

Genetics is the study of people from the same family. Do you have your mother's eye color? Are you tall like your father? Are you shy like your grandfather? Are you good at sports like your grandmother? The way we look—our eye color, hair color, and height—comes from our family. Our personality can also come from our family. Genetics scientists study how people are the same and different within families.

You will listen to

- a presentation about genetics and personality.
- people describing their roommates.
- a class discussion about how hobbies connect to genetics.

You will also

- give a short presentation about a roommate.
- describe three relatives.

For more about **GENETICS**, see Chapter 4. See also RW **GENETICS**, Chapters 3 and 4.

OUTCOMES

- Listen for gist
- Describe people
- Understand and use contractions
- Understand and use antonyms
- Learn how to give great presentations

GETTING STARTED

Look at the photo and the icons. Circle the icons that people get through genetics (from our family).

tall

brown hair

good at music

good student

good at art

good at sports

brown eyes

◉ Go to **MyEnglishLab** to complete a self-assessment.

LISTEN

SKILL: LISTENING FOR GIST

When you listen for the gist, you listen for the general topic or purpose. You do not need listen for details. It is not important to listen to every word. Just focus on one general idea.

To listen for gist, listen for

- the topic in the first sentences.
- words the speaker repeats.
- words that connect to the same topic.

Ask yourself, "What is the speaker talking about?"

🎧 **A. Listen. Complete the tasks.**

1. What is the main topic of the first sentence?

   _____

2. What word does the speaker repeat?

   _____

3. What is the gist? Check (✔) your answer.

   ☐ a. funny movies
   ☐ b. the beach
   ☐ c. his soccer team
   ☐ d. his brother

B. Listen. Complete the tasks.

1. What is the main topic of the first sentence?

   _____

2. What word does the speaker repeat?

   _____

3. What is the gist? (What is the speaker talking about?) Check (✓) your answer.

   ☐ a. family
   ☐ b. hair
   ☐ c. height
   ☐ d. colors

4. Read the information. Circle the other words that relate to the topic.

   > Everyone in my family has different hair. My mother's hair is short and brown. My sister's hair is long and blond. I have short red hair. And my dad doesn't have any hair. He is bald!

REMEMBER

Complete the sentences.

1. When you listen for the gist, you listen for the _____
   or _____ .

2. You do not need to listen for _____ .

3. It is _____ important to listen to every word.

4. To listen for the gist, listen for the _____ in the first sentence, words the speaker _____ , and words that _____ to the same topic.

5. Ask yourself, "_____ ?"

VOCABULARY PREVIEW

A. Read the sentences. Look at the boldfaced words. Do you know what they mean? Share your ideas with a partner.

1. My **grandparents** are tall. My parents are tall, too.

2. Keiko and Kazu are **both** scientists.

3. Abdul has a great **personality**. He is kind and friendly to everyone.

4. My brother always **acts** like my father. They are both loud.

5. My father is very **quiet**. He doesn't talk much.

6. I like this movie. It makes me **laugh**.

7. My parents love **adventure**. They eat different food and go to interesting places.

8. My roommate is **nice**. She cooks dinner for me.

9. My parents **worry** a lot. They think bad things are going to happen.

10. He is very **lazy**. He doesn't do his homework. He watches TV all day.

11. She is 18 years old. She is an **adult** now.

B. Write the boldfaced words from Part A next to their definitions.

_____ 1. doesn't want to work or do anything

_____ 2. make a sound when something is funny

_____ 3. two things or people

_____ 4. doesn't talk a lot

_____ 5. kind

_____ 6. not a child; a grown-up person

_____ 7. behaves in a particular way

_____ 8. feel unhappy or nervous about something

_____ 9. the parents of your parents

_____ 10. a person's character; how he/she behaves

_____ 11. an exciting or unusual experience

(Continued)

C. You will hear these sentences and phrases in the listening. Read them aloud with a partner. Do you remember the meanings of the boldfaced words?

1. When we look at our mothers, fathers, and **grandparents**, we can often see ways that we are the same.

2. Are you and your sister **both** tall or short?

3. Did you know that **personality** traits can come from genetics, too?

4. Your personality is who you are. It is the way you **act** or behave.

5. Maybe you are **quiet** or don't talk much.

6. Maybe you like to **laugh** or maybe you love **adventure**.

7. These are examples of personality traits. Other examples are being a **nice** person.

8. Do you know people who **worry** a lot about problems?

9. If your grandparents are **lazy** and don't like to work, you may act the same way.

10. Children learn these traits by watching the **adults** in their lives.

🔊 Go to **MyEnglishLab** to complete a vocabulary practice.

PREDICT

Look at the pictures. Think about the speaker, the situation, and the topic. Then predict the words and phrases you will hear. Complete the chart.

Personality and Genetics

Speaker	
Situation	
Topic	
Words and Phrases	

LISTEN BEFORE YOU SPEAK

🎧 A. Listen to the presentation. Check (✓) if your predictions are correct or incorrect. For any that are incorrect, write the correct information.

	Correct	Incorrect	Correct Information
Speaker			
Situation			
Topic			
Words and Phrases			

B. Answer the questions.

1. What is the gist (main topic) of the presentation?

_____

2. What words helped you understand the gist?

_____

🎧 C. Listen to the excerpts from the presentation. Read the sentences. Circle *T* (true) or *F* (false). Correct the false statements.

SECTION 1

T / F   1. The gist of this section is personality traits.

_____

T / F   2. We know that physical traits come from genetics.

_____

SECTION 2

T / F   3. The gist of this section is personality traits.

_____

T / F   4. A personality trait is the way we act or behave sometimes.

_____

SECTION 3

T / F   5. Scientists do not believe that personality comes from genetics.

_____

T / F   6. Some scientists think that children learn their personalities from adults.

_____

LISTEN AGAIN

A. Listen again. Circle all of the traits the speaker talks about.

eye color	hair color	like to laugh	shape of face
funny	happy	love adventure	shape of nose
good at art	height (tall or short)	nice	small ears
good at math	large feet	quiet	works hard
good at sports	lazy	sad	worries a lot

B. Check (✓) the sentence that best explains the gist.

☐ 1. Many physical traits come from a person's genetics.

☐ 2. Some scientists believe that personality can come from genetics.

☐ 3. Scientists know that children get their personalities by watching adults.

C. Complete the conversation with your own ideas. Then practice the conversation with five classmates. Take turns with A and B roles.

A: What traits do you share with your family members?

B: My _____ and I are both _____ .

   We both are / have / like _____ .

VOCABULARY REVIEW

Complete the sentences with words from the box.

act	adventure	grandparents	lazy	personality	worry
adult	both	laugh	nice	quiet	

1. My teacher is very _____ ! She always helps us after class.

2. My brothers are _____ . They don't talk much.

3. Being nice and happy are two _____ traits parents pass to children.

4. Junko and Kazu _____ like their parents. They're both funny and friendly.

5. I am an _____ now. My birthday was yesterday, and I am 18 years old.

6. My parents like _____ . They go to many different countries.

7. Do your _____ live near you? My mother's parents live near us.

8. Habib is _____ . He doesn't do any work at school.

9. That movie is funny. I _____ whenever I see it.

10. _____ of my parents like to travel.

11. My parents _____ a lot about me. They think I have problems at school.

↻ Go to **MyEnglishLab** for more listening practice.

SPEAK

SKILL: DESCRIBING PEOPLE

When we describe people, we talk about their traits. We can describe both physical and personality traits. When you know the vocabulary for describing people, you can give more details. Your description will be more interesting.

Describing Physical Traits	Describing Personality Traits
What does he / she **look like**?	What **is** he / she **like**?
What do they **look like**?	What **are** they **like**?
She is tall / short.	**He is** quiet / shy.
He has long hair / short hair / blue eyes.	**She is** nice / smart.
They have brown eyes / nice smiles.	**They are** lazy / funny.

A. Work with a partner. Practice the conversation. Take turns with A and B roles.

A: Tell me about your sister. What does she look like?

B: She is tall and she has brown hair.

A: What is she like?

B: She is nice. She is funny. And she is quiet.

B. Change partners and practice the conversation with two more classmates. Ask about their family members.

REMEMBER

Complete the sentences.

When we talk about people, we describe their _____ . We can describe both physical and _____ traits. When you know the vocabulary for describing people, you can give more _____ . Your description will be more _____ .

Draw a line to match the questions to the details.

What does he look like?   Information about personality

What is he like?   Information about appearance

There are many contractions in English. When we form a contraction, we put two words together. We use an apostrophe (') in place of missing letters, for example, *I am = I'm*.

CONTRACTIONS WITH *BE* (AFFIRMATIVE)

Pronoun	*Be*	Contraction
I	am	I**'m**
You	are	You**'re**
He / She / It	is	He**'s** / She**'s** / It**'s**

CONTRACTIONS WITH *BE* (NEGATIVE)

Pronoun	*Be*	Contraction
I	am not	I**'m** not
You	are not	You**'re** not / You **aren't**
He / She / It	is not	He**'s** not / He **isn't**
I / He / She / It	was not	I **wasn't**
You / We / They	were not	You **weren't**

CONTRACTIONS WITH *DO* (NEGATIVE)

Pronoun	*Do*	Contraction
I / You / We / They	do not	I / You / We / They **don't**
He / She / It	does not	He / She / It **doesn't**

CONTRACTIONS WITH OTHER WORDS + *BE*

Word	*Be*	Contraction
That	is	That**'s**
There	is	There**'s**
What / Who / Where When / How	is	What**'s** / Who**'s** / Where**'s** / When**'s** / How**'s**

GRAMMAR NOTE

We use contractions for informal speaking and informal writing. For example, we use contractions when we speak or write to a friend or a family member. We do not use contractions in formal writing, for example, a research paper or an email message to a professor.

A. Use the words at the end of each line to write a contraction to complete the sentences.

1. My brothers _____ lazy. They work a lot. (are not)

2. Martina _____ an adult. She's only 15 years old. (is not)

3. I _____ like to travel. (do not)

4. _____ your mother's name? (What is)

5. My father _____ like movies. (does not)

6. _____ your grandmother? (Who is)

7. _____ tall like my grandparents. (I am)

8. Li and Keiko _____ travel. (do not)

9. You _____ like your mother. (are not)

10. _____ very nice. (He is)

B. Circle the correct contraction to complete each sentence.

1. (**When's / Where's / There's**) your mother in this picture?

2. The sisters (**aren't / isn't / don't**) the same.

3. My brother (**aren't / don't / doesn't**) travel.

4. My grandparents (**weren't / don't / isn't**) very nice.

5. (**How's / Doesn't / You're**) an adult now.

6. (**Aren't / That's / When's**) my mother in the photo.

7. My brother (**isn't / doesn't / don't**) lazy.

8. My parents (**aren't / isn't / don't**) look the same.

C. Use the words at the end of each line to write a contraction to complete the conversation. Then practice the conversation with a partner.

A: _____ that in the photo? (Who is)
1

B: _____ my mother. (That is)
2

A: _____ she like? (What is)
3

B: _____ nice. She is a doctor. She helps many people. (She is)
4

A: How about your father? _____ he like? (What is)
5

B: _____ quiet. (He is) He _____
6   7
talk much. (does not)

A: What does he look like?

B: _____ very tall. (He is) He has
8
short hair. _____ black. (It is)
9

🔊 **Go to MyEnglishLab for more grammar practice.**

DESCRIBE A ROOMMATE

STEP 1: LISTEN BEFORE YOU SPEAK

A. Look at the picture. Think about the speakers, the situation, and the topic. Then predict the words or phrases that you will hear. Complete the chart.

Speakers	
Situation	
Topic	
Words and Phrases	

B. Read the words and definitions. You will hear these words in the listening.

> **Glossary**
>
> **athletic:** good at sports
>
> **mind (v):** dislike or feel annoyed by something
>
> **early:** before the usual or expected time
>
> **get along:** have a friendly relationship with someone
>
> **hang out:** spend time with someone or in a place
>
> **hardworking:** working hard
>
> **joke:** something funny you say to make people laugh

C. Listen. Complete the tasks.

1. The speakers are talking about _____ .

   a. their relatives   b. nice classmates   c. their roommates

2. You need a roommate. Which person do you choose? Circle your choice. Then find a partner and share your answer and your reasons. Use the examples to help you.

Gabriella

Pablo

Chen

I want to live with …

She / He is …

We both like …

STEP 2: PREPARE TO SPEAK

A. You are going to give a short presentation to describe a roommate. Read the audio scripts from Step 1. Follow these instructions:

1. Underline the words that describe physical traits.
2. Circle the words that describe personality traits.
3. Draw a box around the contractions.

1. I have a nice roommate this year. Her name is Gabriella. She's from Poland. She has long, black hair and she has brown eyes. She's very quiet and hardworking. She studies in the library after class. Then she goes to sleep early. I don't see her very often, but she's nice.

2. I like my roommate a lot. He's interesting! His name is Pablo. He's from Colombia. He's tall and very athletic. He plays every sport. We play basketball every weekend. We also both like music a lot. We get along well. I'm happy he's my roommate.

3. My roommate this year is very funny. His name is Chen and he's from Hong Kong. He's short, like me. He tells lots of jokes. Sometimes he's loud, but I don't mind. We both like movies. It's fun to hang out with him. We laugh a lot.

B. Plan your presentation. If you have a roommate, describe him or her. If you don't have a roommate, imagine the person. Think about their traits and interests. Use ideas from the box or think of your own. Write sentences to describe your roommate. Use contractions in your sentences.

Physical Traits	Personality Traits		Interests and Hobbies
He / She is … tall / short	**He / She is …** athletic	quiet	**He / she likes … / is good at …** sports music art movies
He / She has … long / short hair blond / brown / black / red hair brown / blue / green eyes	hardworking interesting loud nice	funny happy helpful	**He / she likes to …** study laugh help read cook tell jokes watch TV talk play (basketball, chess, soccer, tennis, video games)

> My roommate
>
> He is tall. He has green eyes. He is funny. He likes to make people laugh.
>
> 1. _____
> 2. _____
> 3. _____
> 4. _____
> 5. _____

C. Work with a partner. Share your sentences. Help each other correct any errors.

STEP 3: SPEAK

A. Practice your description. Remember to look up when you speak and to smile.

B. Work in a group. Take turns describing your roommates. Use the examples to help you.

> My roommate is …
>
> He's / She's …
>
> He / She likes (to) …
>
> I like my roommate a lot because he / she …

STEP 4: PEER FEEDBACK

Write the names of three classmates in the first column. Listen to their descriptions. Write the personality traits they describe.

Classmates	Personality Traits
Gabriella	quiet, hardworking

BUILDING VOCABULARY

UNDERSTANDING AND USING ANTONYMS

Antonyms are words that have the opposite (not the same) meaning, for example, *bad / good*; *up / down*. Learning antonyms can help you remember new vocabulary better. Antonyms can also help you describe people, places, and things in more detail.

A. Read the pairs of antonyms from the box. Do you know what all of the words mean? Share your ideas with a partner. Then think of another pair of antonyms and write it in the box.

short / tall	lazy / hardworking	small / big	funny / serious
nice / mean	interesting / boring	loud / quiet	_____

B. Label each photo or pair of photos with the antonyms from Part A.

_____

_____

_____

_____

_____

_____

C. Complete the conversations with an antonym from the box in Part A.
Then practice reading the conversations with a partner.

1. A: My grandparents are very funny.
   B: Mine aren't. My grandparents are very _____ .

2. A: My class is very quiet.
   B: Mine isn't. My class is very _____ .

3. A: My brothers are tall.
   B: Mine aren't. My brothers are _____ .

4. A: That book is very interesting.
   B: I don't think so. I think it's _____ .

5. A: My roommate is lazy.
   B: Mine isn't. My roommate is _____ .

6. A: My teacher is nice.
   B: Mine isn't. My teacher is _____ .

7. A: I'm small.
   B: I'm not. I'm _____ .

D. Write three short conversations using antonyms. Practice the conversations
with a partner. Then choose one to perform for the class.

🔵 Go to **MyEnglishLab** to complete a vocabulary practice.

APPLY YOUR SKILLS

In this chapter, you listened to a podcast about personality traits. You listened to students describe their roommates and you described a roommate. In Apply Your Skills, you will listen to a classroom discussion about how our hobbies and careers can come from genetics. You will give a short talk about three family members and how their personality traits relate to their hobbies.

VOCABULARY PREVIEW

A. Read the sentences. Look at the boldfaced words and phrases. Do you know what they mean? Share your ideas with a partner.

1. Our black hair **comes from** our grandparents. They're from Mexico.

2. She and her father have the same **career**. They are both teachers.

3. An **example** of a hobby is cooking.

4. She is **probably** his sister. They have the same face.

5. Your **relatives** are tall. Your mother, father, and grandparents are all tall.

6. My grandparents were farmers in 1936. That was many years **ago**.

7. **All** the people in my family have brown eyes.

8. My mother and I have the same **interests**. We both like to travel.

9. My brother has many **skills**. He learned them from our father.

10. Many times people **choose** the same career as their father or mother.

B. Write the boldfaced words from Part A next to their definitions.

_____ 1. things you like to do

_____ 2. decide what you want from a group of things or people

_____ 3. in the past

_____ 4. one thing that you tell about to show what the other things are like

_____ 5. likely to happen or to be true

_____ 6. the whole of something

_____ 7. starts from a place

_____ 8. a job you know a lot about and you do for a long time

_____ 9. activities you can do well

_____ 10. family members

🔊 Go to **MyEnglishLab** to complete a vocabulary practice.

PREDICT

Look at the photos. Think about the speaker, the situation, and the topic. Then predict the words or phrases that you will hear. Complete the chart.

Speaker	
Situation	
Topic	
Words and Phrases	

LISTEN

A. Listen to the lecture. Check (✓) your predictions. Were they correct? Which ones? Tell a partner.

My prediction was correct / incorrect about …

B. Check (✓) the gist of the lecture.

☐ 1. interesting hobbies and careers

☐ 2. genetics and physical traits

☐ 3. genetics and careers and hobbies

☐ 4. genetics of plants and flowers

C. Listen to the excerpts from the lecture. Choose the correct answers.

SECTION 1

1. What does the study in Britain say?
   a. Over 2,234 people in Britain have hobbies.
   b. Our hobbies and careers come from genetics.
   c. It's important for families to have hobbies.

SECTION 2

2. An example of the hobby gene is a good cook who _____.
   a. learned how to cook in school
   b. works in a family restaurant
   c. probably has a relative who liked to cook

3. The hobby gene only comes from your mother or father.
   a. True   b. False

4. The hobby gene says that you may not have the same career, but you may have _____.
   a. the same skills as a relative
   b. the same interests as a relative
   c. Both a and b

5. Great-great-grandparents are _____.
   a. parents of your grandparents
   b. grandparents of your grandparents
   c. parents of your great grandparents

6. We always have the same career and hobby as our parents.
   a. True   b. False

LISTEN AGAIN

A. Listen again. Complete the sentences with words from the box.

careers	genetics	interests	probably	skills

1. Scientists say that hobbies and careers come from _____ .

2. Someone who likes to cook _____ has a relative who also likes to cook.

3. We often have the same _____ as our relatives. For example, teachers often have a relative who is or was a teacher.

4. Some careers have the same _____ .

5. We are born with the skills and _____ of our family.

B. Circle and write information to complete the conversations about yourself. Then practice the conversations with a partner.

1. A: How do you think people choose their careers?

   B: I think most people choose a career because of their (**interests / skills / relatives**).

2. A: Do you and your relatives have the same hobbies or interests?

   B: Yes, my (**mother / father / sister / brother**) and I both _____ .

   OR

   B: No, we don't have the same hobbies or interests. I like _____ , but my _____ .

3. A: Do you and your relatives have the same career?

   B: Yes, I have the same career as my _____ . We both _____ .

   OR

   B: No, we don't have the same career. I _____ , but my _____ .

C. Work in a group. Discuss the questions.

1. In what ways are your family members the same? How are they different?

2. Do you think that our hobbies and interests come from our genes? Give examples from your family.

VOCABULARY REVIEW

Complete the sentences with words and phrases from the box.

ago	career	come from	interests	relatives
all	choose	example	probably	skill

1. She has the same _____ as her mother. They're both nurses.

2. Scientists say that personality and physical traits _____ from genetics.

3. My grandparents and I have the same _____ . We like to plant flowers.

4. Speaking English is an important _____ for my job.

5. My grandparents were teachers a long time _____ .

6. The baby's parents are tall. She's _____ going to be tall, too.

7. Many people _____ their jobs because of their **family**.

8. _____ my brothers and sisters are tall.

9. An _____ of a career is teaching.

10. My _____ were all farmers. My grandparents **had a farm**.

THINK VISUALLY

Look at the chart. Answer the questions.

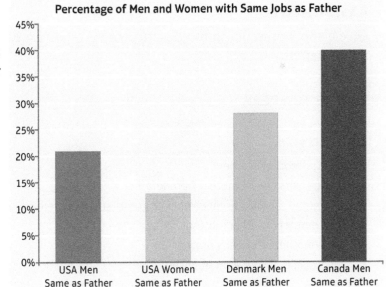

Percentage of Men and Women with Same Jobs as Father

1. In which country do 40 percent of the men have the same career as their father?
   a. USA
   b. Denmark
   c. Canada

2. What percentage of men in the USA have the same career as their father?
   a. 28%
   b. 13%
   c. 40%
   d. 22%

3. What percentage of men in Denmark have the same career as their father?
   a. 28%   b. 13%   c. 40%   d. 22%

4. In which country do 28 percent of the men have the same job as their father?
   a. USA   b. Denmark   c. Canada

5. How many countries are represented in the chart?
   a. one   b. two   c. three

GRAMMAR

USING CONTRACTIONS

**Read the conversation. Find and change 11 phrases into contractions.
Then practice the conversation with a partner.**

Ahmed: Hi, Rafael. What are you doing?

Rafael: Hi, Ahmed. I am looking at pictures of my family.

Ahmed: Can I see them?

Rafael: Sure.

Ahmed: Who is that?

Rafael: That is my grandfather. And over here is my grandmother.

Ahmed: They are your grandparents? They are not very old! Where are they from?

Rafael: He is Brazilian, and she is from Japan.

Ahmed: Interesting! What do they do?

Rafael: They are cooks. They have a restaurant together. He is very good at making Mexican food. She is good at making desserts.

Ahmed: Interesting. So, that is why you are good at cooking!

ASSIGNMENT

Give a short presentation to describe three relatives. Explain the ways you are the same and different.

PREPARE TO SPEAK

Glossary

parents: mother / father

grandparents: grandmother / grandfather

great-grandparents: grandmother or grandfather's parents

aunt: mother or father's sister

uncle: mother or father's brother

cousin: child of your aunt or uncle

A. Think of three of your relatives.

B. Think of ways you and your relatives from Part A are the same or different. Use these ideas or add your own.

Physical Traits	Personality Traits	Hobbies	Careers
hair color	athletic	traveling	teacher
eye color	funny / serious	gardening	nurse
height (tall, short)	lazy / hardworking	cooking	doctor
size (big, small)	nice / mean	music	computer engineer
_____	quiet / loud	art	chef
_____	interesting / boring	sports	writer
	_____	_____	musician
	_____	_____	farmer
			_____
			_____

C. Complete the chart about your three relatives. Use contractions and antonyms when you can.

Name / Relative	Ways You Are the Same	Ways You Are Different
Yasmin / Mother	We both have blond hair. We are both athletic. We both like gardening.	She's funny, but I'm serious. She likes to cook, but I don't.

D. Work with a partner. Choose one relative from Part C. Take turns practicing your presentation. Show a picture of your relative (if you have one). Use the examples to help you.

I'm going to talk about my …

We are the same because we both …

We are the different because he / she … but I …

SPEAK

A. Give your presentation to the class. Use the examples to help you.

First, I'm going to talk about my …

We are the same because we both …

We are the different because he / she … but I …

Next, I'm going to talk about my …

Finally, I'm going to talk about my …

B. Listen to your classmates' presentations. Choose three classmates and write their names in the chart and write one detail about each relative.

Classmates' Names	Relative	Details

Go to **MyEnglishLab** to complete grammar and vocabulary practices.

DEVELOP SOFT SKILLS

GIVING GREAT PRESENTATIONS

Part of university study is giving presentations. As a student, you need to learn how to present well. For some people, giving presentations is scary. You have to stand and speak in front of many people. How can you make this easier? Don't worry! You just need practice.

> **Glossary**
>
> prepare: make something ready
>
> nervous: worried or afraid
>
> audience: the people watching a presentation
>
> eye contact: looking at someone else's eyes

A. Answer the questions. Then compare answers in a group.

1. How easy or hard is it for you to give presentation in your language? Mark your answer on the line.

Easy   Hard

2. How easy or hard is it for you to give presentation in English? Mark your answer on the line.

Easy   Hard

3. How do you prepare for a presentation? Check (✓) the things you do.

☐ ask a friend to watch and listen

☐ check pronunciation of difficult words

☐ make a recording of the presentation

☐ make a video of yourself

☐ practice

☐ time the presentation

☐ write out the whole presentation

4. What makes a presentation good? Circle your ideas.

interesting topic	good eye contact	easy to understand
nice pictures	good speaker	your idea: _____

B. Listen to two students, Vlad and Binnu, talking about about preparing for a presentation. Answer the questions.

1. Does Vlad know the topic of his presentation well? _____

2. Why does Binnu think it is a bad idea to read the whole presentation?

_____

3. How many times does Binnu say to practice? _____

4. What ideas does Binnu give for practicing the presentation?

_____

_____

C. Listen to the online video about good presentations. What advice does the speaker give? Take notes.

_____

_____

_____

D. Listen again. Complete the list of Dos and Don'ts the speaker gives.

Do	Don't
• take notes • practice	• write out the whole presentation

E. Prepare a one-minute presentation about a famous person you know. Describe their physical and personality traits, career, interests, and hobbies. Do not say the person's name or show their picture. Use ideas from the unit to help you.

- Make note cards with only the main ideas and important details.
- Practice. Ask some friends to watch.

F. Give your presentation to the class. Can your classmates guess who you are talking about?

WHAT DID YOU LEARN?

Check (✓) the skills and vocabulary you learned. Circle the things you need to practice.

SKILLS

☐ I can listen for gist.

☐ I can describe people.

☐ I can understand and use contractions.

☐ I can understand and use antonyms.

☐ I can give great presentations.

VOCABULARY

☐ act

☐ adult

☐ adventure

☐ ago

☐ all

☐ both

☐ career

☐ choose

☐ come from

☐ example

☐ grandparents

☐ interest

☐ laugh

☐ lazy

☐ nice

☐ personality

☐ probably

☐ quiet

☐ relative

☐ same

☐ skill

☐ worry

🔾 Go to **MyEnglishLab** to complete a self-assessment.

Chapter 4 How We Learn

CHAPTER PROFILE

Genetics is about the traits we get from our family—the way we look and the type of person we are.

You will listen to

• a lecture about genetics and learning.

• short presentations about learning styles.

• a discussion about genetics and language learning.

You will also

• give a short presentation about your learning style.

• suggest language learning activities.

OUTCOMES

• Listen for examples

• Express degrees of like and dislike

• Use *like* + infinitive verb forms

• Identify and use collocations

• Know your personal learning style

For more about **GENETICS**, see Chapter 3. See also |RW| **GENETICS**, Chapters 3 and 4.

GETTING STARTED

A. Work with a partner. Look at the photos. Read the ways people learn. Write the numbers of the pictures next to the ways people learn in the chart below.

Ways People Learn	
_____ alone	_____ listening
_____ with other people	_____ speaking/discussing
_____ in a busy place	_____ reading
_____ in a quiet place	_____ writing
_____ drawing pictures	_____ sitting
_____ doing / building	_____ moving around

B. How do you like to learn? Circle the ways from the box in Part A. Then compare with a partner.

⬆ Go to **MyEnglishLab** to complete a self-assessment.

LISTEN

SKILL: LISTENING FOR EXAMPLES

Examples are a type of detail. Speakers often use examples to make their ideas clear. Examples connect the topic to information, facts, or events in real life. When you can listen for examples, you can connect the topic to what you know. This helps you understand better.

Speakers often use these phrases to introduce examples:

For example, …   One of these is …

For instance, …   Such as …

An example of this is …   Like …

One / Another / One more example is …

A. Listen to the lecture. Check (✓) the examples the speaker gives about physical traits and personality.

Physical Traits (the Way We Look)	Personality
☐ eye color	Being …
☐ hair color	☐ a good student
☐ skin color	☐ good at sports
☐ height	☐ shy
☐ weight	☐ kind
☐ body shape	☐ funny
	☐ good at music

B. Listen to the lecture again. Check (✓) the phrases the speaker uses to introduce examples.

☐ For example, …   ☐ For instance, …

☐ One of these is …   ☐ Like …

☐ Another example of this is …   ☐ One more example is …

☐ Such as …

C. Listen. Circle the phrases you hear.

People learn in different ways. The way you learn is called your learning style. Some people learn best when they can *see* the information in pictures, (**such as / like**) drawings or diagrams. (**One example / Another example**) is watching videos. Other people learn best by *hearing* information, (**for instance, / for example,**) listening to lectures or presentations.

REMEMBER

Complete the missing information.

Examples are a type of _____ .

Speakers often use examples to make their ideas _____ .

When you can listen for examples, you can connect the topic to

_____ .

Speakers often use these phrases to introduce examples:

_____   _____

_____   _____

_____   _____

_____

VOCABULARY PREVIEW

A. Read the sentences. Look at the boldfaced words and phrases. Do you know what they mean? Share your ideas with a partner.

1. I learn **best** when I talk about the information with other students.
2. The students **discuss** the topic in class. They talk about their ideas.
3. I don't **remember** all of the information from the lecture.
4. I don't **take notes** in class. It is difficult for me to write fast.
5. I **need** a quiet space to do my schoolwork.
6. One **way** to learn is to watch videos.
7. The teachers **let** the students work together.
8. They can **choose** to write sentences or give a presentation.
9. The teacher gives a lot of **homework**. I do it in the library after school
10. The students were **successful** in class. They did very well.

B. Write the boldfaced words and phrases from Part A next to their definitions.

_____ 1. allow someone to do something

_____ 2. not forget something; to keep the information in your head

_____ 3. write information on paper or in a computer

_____ 4. decide between different things

_____ 5. doing something very well

_____ 6. how to do something

_____ 7. feel that you must have something

_____ 8. talk about something with someone

_____ 9. schoolwork to do at home or after class

_____ 10. better than any other

C. You will hear these sentences in the listening. Read them aloud with a partner. Do you remember the meanings of the boldfaced words and phrases?

1. How do you learn **best**?
2. Do you like to listen to lectures? **Discuss** your ideas?
3. What helps you **remember** information?
4. Do you like to **take notes**?
5. He **needs** to learn in a quiet **way**, like reading or writing.
6. An example of this is when teachers **let** students **choose** how to learn.
7. For **homework**, for example, students can read about a topic, or they can listen to a lecture online.
8. This way genetics helps teachers understand how to help every student be **successful**.

🔊 Go to **MyEnglishLab** to complete a vocabulary practice.

PREDICT

Look at the pictures. Think about the speaker, the situation, and the topic. Then predict the words and phrases you will hear. Complete the chart.

Speaker	
Situation	
Topic	
Words and Phrases	

LISTEN BEFORE YOU SPEAK

A. Listen to the presentation. Check (✓) if your predictions are correct or incorrect. For any that are incorrect, write the correct information.

	Correct	Incorrect	Correct Information
Speaker			
Situation			
Topic			
Words and Phrases			

B. Check (✓) the main idea of the lecture.

☐ 1. Students study in different ways.

☐ 2. Most students don't like to read or write.

☐ 3. Genetics may help students learn better.

☐ 4. Teachers don't know how to teach genetics.

C. Listen to the excerpts from the lecture. Circle the correct information.

SECTION 1

1. Each of us has a different way of (**reading / learning / teaching**).

2. Some scientists say our learning style may come from our (**schools / teachers / genes**).

SECTION 2

3. Research shows that people in the same (**class / family / house**) may have the same learning style.

4. Some people learn best with their (**hands / friends / books**), for example, building, drawing, or making art.

5. If your grandfather does not like to talk much, you may learn best by (**discussing in class / reading or writing / working with your hands**).

SECTION 3

6. Educational genomics uses (**teachers / genetics / tests**) to find out a person's learning style.

7. Scientists give this information to the (**parents / students / schools**).

8. Teachers let students choose (**how they learn / what they read / how many tests they take**).

9. When students take a test, they do it (**the same way / in different ways / at home**).

LISTEN AGAIN

A. Listen again. Circle *T* (true) or *F* (false). Correct the false statements.

T / F 1. Most students like to learn in the same way.

_____

T / F 2. Some teachers let their students choose how to learn.

_____

T / F 3. There are many different learning styles.

_____

T / F 4. Research shows that learning styles may come from genetics.

_____

T / F 5. Some scientists say that we are born with our learning styles.

_____

T / F 6. It is best for teachers to teach all students the same way.

_____

B. Complete the sentences with words from the box.

build	discuss	draw	learn	learning styles	listen	teachers

1. Educational genomics suggests that we are born with our _____ .

2. Genetics may help _____ know more about their students' learning styles.

3. Some students like to _____ to a lecture or a talk.

4. Some students like to _____ pictures, such as diagrams or graphs.

5. Some students like to _____ the topic with other students.

6. Some teachers let their students choose how they _____ .

7. People who like to work with their hands like to _____ things or make art.

C. Talk with a partner. Do you think you have the same learning style as your family members? Who? Why do you think so?

I think I am like my father. We both like to … We are both good at …

VOCABULARY REVIEW

Complete the sentences with words and phrases from the box.

best	discuss	let	remember	take notes
choose	homework	need	successful	ways

1. I _____ a quiet place to learn. I do better in a quiet space.

2. My mother and I don't like to write. We don't like to _____ in class.

3. My friends and I _____ the topic at lunch time. We talk about many things.

4. The teacher gives us different _____ to show what we learned in class.

5. Genetics may help students be _____ in class.

6. I _____ vocabulary words when I write them. I forget them when I just look at the words.

7. My teachers _____ students work together in class.

8. Stefan can't go to dinner with us tonight. He has a lot of _____ .

9. I like to work with my hands. I learn _____ when I do the skill for myself.

10. Students learn best when teachers let them _____ their own way to learn.

◐ Go to **MyEnglishLab** for more listening practice.

SPEAK

SKILL: EXPRESSING DEGREES OF LIKE AND DISLIKE

There are different ways to talk about likes and dislikes. You can explain the degree—how much—you like or dislike something. When you use different expressions, you can express your feelings more clearly. And your English will sound more natural.

Use these phrases to express the degree of like or dislike.

DEGREES OF LIKE

–   +

I kind of like …   I like …   I really like …   I love …

DEGREES OF DISLIKE

–   +

I don't really like …   I don't like …   I can't stand …   I hate …

A. Listen. Complete the missing parts of the conversation. Then practice the conversation with a partner.

Angela: You start classes soon, Miguel. Are you going to the same college as your brother, José?

Miguel: Yes. I'm going to City University, too.

Angela: That's great! You and José can study together!

Miguel: No, I don't think so. We are very different. He _____
1
listen to loud music when he studies.

Angela: You _____ music?
2

Miguel: I _____ music. But I _____ noise.
3   4
I need quiet when I study.

Angela: I see.

Miguel: José also _____ to talk to his friends on the phone.
5
He often calls them to discuss ideas.

Angela: Well, maybe you can discuss ideas with him.

Miguel: I _____ my brother,
6
but I _____ to
7
study alone.

B. Think of a family member. Write sentences to compare your likes and dislikes about each topic. Use expressions for degrees of like and dislike. Use the example to help you.

1. (hobbies) *I love sports. My sister can't stand sports.* _____
2. (music) _____
3. (food) _____
4. (TV shows) _____
5. (school subjects) _____
6. (learning styles) _____

REMEMBER

Write the expressions for degrees of like and dislike along the line. Write the words that express extreme like or dislike on either end, and then write the other words in order of degrees on the line.

DEGREES OF LIKE

–   +

_____ _____ _____ _____

DEGREES OF DISLIKE

–   +

_____ _____ _____ _____

Grammar for Speaking Using *like* + infinitive verb forms

An infinitive is the form of a verb that starts with *to,* for example, *to go, to study, to make* we use *like* or *don't like* + infinitive to express likes and dislikes about different activities.

	Like + infinitive	Examples
Affirmative	I / You / We / They **like to** _____ . He / She / It **likes to** _____ .	• I **like to study** in the library. • He **likes to watch** the teacher do it first.
Negative	I / You / We / They **don't like to** _____ . He / She / It **doesn't like to** _____ .	• They **don't like to take** notes. • She **doesn't like to discuss** the topics.
Question	**Do** you / they **like to** _____ ? **Does** he / she **like to** _____ ?	• Do you **like to see** a chart? • Does she **like to listen** to lectures?

GRAMMAR NOTE

You can use expressions for degrees of like and dislike with infinitive forms, too. For instance,

She **hates to study** alone.　　　　　That teacher **really likes to** show videos in class.

We **love to meet** at this coffee shop.　　I **kind of like to give** presentations.

A. Circle the correct answer.

1. The students _____ watch movies in class.
   a. like to
   b. likes to
   c. doesn't like to

2. My teacher _____ give us different ways to do our homework.
   a. like to
   b. don't like to
   c. likes to

3. Sam _____ study in a quiet room.
   a. like to
   b. don't like to
   c. doesn't like to

4. Kathryn and James _____ discuss the topics after class.
   a. like to
   b. does like to
   c. likes to

5. _____ you and your brother like to study together?
   a. Do
   b. Does
   c. Doesn't

6. The teachers at our school _____ give a lot of homework.
   a. like to
   b. likes to
   c. doesn't like to

7. He _____ move around when he studies.
   a. like to
   b. likes to
   c. does like to

8. _____ your father like to listen to lectures?
   a. Do
   b. Does
   c. Don't

9. My sister and I have the same learning style. We _____ study with other people.
   a. doesn't like to
   b. does like to
   c. don't like to

B. Write the words in the correct order.

1. to / Ana / listen / music / to / likes / studies / she / when

_____.

2. students / to / the / discuss / the / like / topics / don't

_____.

3. they / to / read / like / write / and / do

_____?

4. likes / teacher / to / my / us / three / give / ways / do / to / homework / the

_____.

5. go / to / we / library / like / the / to

_____.

6. teacher / music / to / the / like / play / class / in / doesn't

_____.

7. brother / to / like / your / talk / topics / the / about / does

_____?

8. Martin / and / to / Nila / presentations / like / give

_____.

9. partner / and / like / together / to / I / my / our / do / homework

_____.

10. Jacques / don't / to / mother / the / way / in / same / his / and / like / study

_____.

C. Use phrases from the box to write five questions. Then ask your partner the questions. Use the example to help you.

discuss / ideas	listen to music / study	study / library
draw pictures / learn	move around / in class	study / on a computer
give presentations / in class	study / coffee shop	take notes / listen

study / quiet place   Do you like to study in a quiet place?

1. _____?

2. _____?

3. _____?

4. _____?

5. _____?

🔾 Go to **MyEnglishLab** for more grammar practice.

PRESENT ABOUT YOUR LEARNING STYLE

STEP 1: LISTEN BEFORE YOU SPEAK

A. Look at the picture. Think about the speakers, the situation, and the topic. Then predict the words and phrases you will hear. Complete the chart.

Campus radio

Speakers	
Situation	
Topic	
Words and Phrases	

B. Read the words and definitions. You will hear these words in the interview.

Glossary

shy: quiet, not liking to be around a lot of people

alone: by yourself, without other people

social: liking to be around and talk to other people

classmates: other students in your class

review: read and study again

visual: something that you can see or look at

CULTURE NOTE

Most college campuses in the United States have their own radio stations. Students can work at the station. They announce campus news, give interviews, and play music.

C. Listen to the radio interviews. Complete the tasks.

Interview 1

1. Check (✓) the correct topic.
   The radio show is about _____ .
   - ☐ a. students from different countries
   - ☐ b. different learning styles and study habits
   - ☐ c. how students like to take tests

2. Check (✓) all of the details that are true.
   - ☐ a. Anika is from Saudi Arabia.
   - ☐ b. She is a shy person.
   - ☐ c. She doesn't like to study alone.
   - ☐ d. Anika likes to take notes in class.
   - ☐ e. There are not many quiet spaces on campus.
   - ☐ f. Anika likes to study in a coffee shop.
   - ☐ g. She loves to go to the library.

3. Check (✔) all of the details that are true.
   - ☐ a. Tomas is from Mexico.
   - ☐ b. He is a social person.
   - ☐ c. He likes to study in quiet places.
   - ☐ d. Tomas can't stand the library.
   - ☐ e. He likes to go to the coffee shop.
   - ☐ f. He likes to study with other people.
   - ☐ g. Tomas and his classmates don't like to discuss their ideas.

Interview 3

4. Check (✔) all of the details that are true.
   - ☐ a. Brendan is from Canada.
   - ☐ b. He is a visual learner.
   - ☐ c. Brendan doesn't like to read or write.
   - ☐ d. He hates tests.
   - ☐ e. He doesn't like to build or make things
   - ☐ f. He likes to draw pictures about what he learned.

STEP 2: PREPARE TO SPEAK

A. Think about how you like to learn. In each pair of activities, check (✔) the one that helps you learn best.

☐ study alone	☐ listen to a lecture	☐ take notes
☐ work with other people	☐ read a book	☐ draw diagrams
☐ build or make something	☐ go to a busy place	☐ write my ideas
☐ write a report	☐ go to a quiet place	☐ discuss my ideas
☐ give a presentation	☐ move around	☐ see information
☐ take a test	☐ sit and listen	☐ hear information

B. Work with a partner. Discuss your answers from Part A. Use the example to help you.

A: Do you like to study alone?

B: Yes, I love to study alone. How about you?

A: I don't really like to study alone. I like to work with other people.

C. Read these descriptions of learning styles. Circle the one(s) that match your learning style. Then compare your answers with a partner.

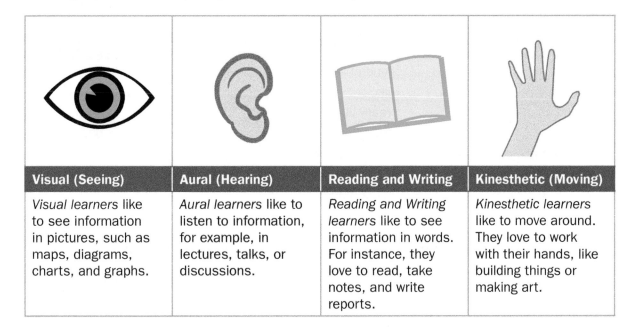

Visual (Seeing)	Aural (Hearing)	Reading and Writing	Kinesthetic (Moving)
Visual learners like to see information in pictures, such as maps, diagrams, charts, and graphs.	*Aural learners* like to listen to information, for example, in lectures, talks, or discussions.	*Reading and Writing learners* like to see information in words. For instance, they love to read, take notes, and write reports.	*Kinesthetic learners* like to move around. They love to work with their hands, like building things or making art.

D. Work in a group of three. Take turns reading aloud the interviews from Step 1. Which type of learner from Part C is each person? Give examples from the interview.

Anika: I'm a shy person. I don't really like to study with other people. I like to study alone. I love to write, so I take a lot of notes in class. Later, I find a quiet space to study my notes. For example, my dormitory has a study lounge on every floor. I also love to go to the library. It has quiet rooms in the back of the building.

Tomas: I am a very social person. I love to be near people. I don't like quiet places. I need a busy place to study. Some students really like the library, but I can't stand it. I like to go to the campus coffee shop. I go with my classmates after class. We review our notes. Then we love to discuss our ideas. Sometimes we stay there until very late.

Brendan: I am a visual learner. So, I love to see the information in a picture, like a chart or a diagram. I don't really like to read or write, so I hate tests. I like to work with my hands, for instance, I like to build or make things. I love to draw. It helps me remember information. For example, after I listen to a lecture or read for homework, I draw a picture or a diagram about what I learned.

E. Plan a short presentation about your learning style. Choose your learning style(s). In the space below, write five examples of how you like to learn. Use the chart to help you. Then circle your learning style(s).

Phrases for Introducing	Degrees of Like and Dislike	Like / Don't Like + Infinitive	
For example …	kind of like		sit
For instance, …	like		read
such as …	really like	like to	listen
like	love	don't like to	build
An example of this is …	don't really like		write
	don't like		make
	can't stand		
	hate		

I think I am a (**visual / aural / reading and writing / kinesthetic**) learner.

1. _____

2. _____

3. _____

4. _____

5. _____

STEP 3: SPEAK

A. Practice your presentation. Remember to look up when you speak and to smile.

B. Give your short presentation to a group of three classmates.

STEP 4: PEER FEEDBACK

Write the names of three classmates in your group in the first column. Then listen to their presentations. Write 1–2 details about how each classmate likes to learn. Use the example to help you.

Classmates	How They Like to Learn
Tonya	loves to talk to classmates, likes to study online

BUILDING VOCABULARY

IDENTIFYING AND USING COLLOCATIONS

A *collocation* is two or more words that often go together. For example, *take notes.* The word *notes* usually has the verb *take* with it. Many times a collocation is verb + noun. There are many collocations with the verbs *take* and *do.*

A. Label the photos with collocations from the box.

do homework	do exercise	take a class	take a test
do research	take a break	take a photo	take notes

1 _____ 2 _____ 3 _____ 4 _____

5 _____ 6 _____ 7 _____ 8 _____

B. Complete the conversations with collocations from Part A. Then practice reading the conversations with a partner.

1. A: Sometimes it's hard to _____ notes in class.
   B: Yes, the teacher talks fast.

2. A: I usually _____ my homework on Sunday afternoons.
   B: I do, too.

3. A: I don't like to _____ a test on Mondays.
   B: Me, either.

4. A: Our teacher lets us _____ a break outside of the classroom.
   B: That's nice.

5. A: I don't really like to _____ a class on Friday afternoons.
   B: I don't, either.

6. A: My parents tell me I need to _____ every day to be healthy.
   B: That's great!

7. A: I am a visual learner, so I like to _____ a photo of the information.
   B: That's a good idea.

8. A: On Fridays, we go to the library to _____ research.
   B: That's a quiet place.

C. Write a short conversation like the ones in Part B. Use collocations. Practice the conversation with a partner. Then share it with the class.

🔊 Go to **MyEnglishLab** to complete a vocabulary practice.

APPLY YOUR SKILLS

In this chapter, you listened to a lecture about how genetics helps people learn. You also listened to three students talk about how they like to learn. Then you gave a short presentation about how you like to learn. In Apply Your Skills, you will listen to a discussion about genetics and language and suggest a language learning activity.

VOCABULARY PREVIEW

A. Read the sentences. Look at the boldfaced words and phrases. Do you know what they mean? Share your ideas with a partner.

1. My school has two **foreign** language classes—Spanish and French.

2. It is **difficult** for some students to learn a language.

3. Some people have an easy time learning the language. They **pick up** the words just by listening to them one time!

4. I like to **practice** my new vocabulary words by playing a game.

5. I **hope** the teacher lets us do our English homework together.

6. My teacher believes that it is good to help others. We have the same **opinion**.

7. It is **helpful** to study with friends.

B. Write the boldfaced words and phrases from Part A next to their definitions.

_____ 1. useful; a good idea

_____ 2. do something often to improve your skill or ability

_____ 3. want something to happen or be true

_____ 4. not easy to do or understand

_____ 5. your ideas or beliefs about something

_____ 6. from a country that is not your country

_____ 7. learn something quickly and easily

🔊 Go to **MyEnglishLab** to complete a vocabulary practice.

PREDICT

Look at the pictures. Think about the speakers, the situation, and the topic. Then predict the words and phrases you will hear. Complete the chart.

Language Learning and Genetics

Speakers	
Situation	
Topic	
Words and Phrases	

LISTEN

A. Listen. Were your predictions correct? Which ones? Tell a partner. Use the example to help you.

My prediction was correct / incorrect about …

B. Check (✓) the main idea of the discussion.

☐ 1. Language learning is difficult for everyone.

☐ 2. Genetics may help people learn languages easily.

☐ 3. It is important to practice words in a new language.

☐ 4. Students from China went to the University of Washington.

☐ 5. Only people with the COMT gene can learn languages.

C. Listen to the excerpts. Read the sentences. Circle *T* (true) or *F* (false). Correct the false statements.

SECTION 1

T / F   1. Anyone can pick up a language in a short time.

_____

T / F   2. It takes a long time for the interviewer to learn a foreign language.

_____

SECTION 2

T / F   3. The study showed that language learning connects to genetics.

_____

T / F   4. The students in the study were from Canada.

_____

T / F   5. Scientists took pictures of the students' faces after the class.

_____

T / F   6. The students with the COMT gene learned more of the language.

_____

SECTION 3

T / F   7. Dr. Levenson thinks that anyone can learn anything.

_____

T / F   8. Dr. Levenson gives some ideas to help with language learning.

_____

T / F   9. Dr. Levenson believes that not everyone can be successful.

_____

T / F   10. Dr. Abaza agrees with Dr. Levenson.

_____

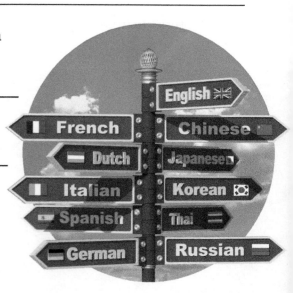

LISTEN AGAIN

🎧 A. Listen again. Complete the passage with words and phrases from the box.

gene	language	pictures	study
genetics	pick up	practice	

Scientists say _____ 1 may help some people learn languages easily. Some of us can _____ 2 languages quickly. But other people need a lot of time and _____ 3 . A _____ 4 at the University of Washington showed that people who have the COMT _____ 5 learn languages better than other people. Students from China took a _____ 6 class. After the class, scientists took _____ 7 of the students' brains. The students who had the COMT gene learned more than the other students.

B. Work with a partner. Discuss these questions.

1. Is it easy or difficult for you to learn a foreign language? What kinds of things help you learn?

2. Do you think everyone can be successful learning a language?

3. What do you suggest for someone who has a difficult time learning English?

VOCABULARY REVIEW
Complete the sentences with words and phrases from the box.

difficult	helpful	opinion	practice
foreign	hope	pick up	

1. Playing games is a _____ way to study vocabulary.

2. My friend and I like to _____ English by watching American movies.

3. I _____ to take an Italian class next year.

4. I think learning grammar is _____ .

5. Ingrid and Rebekah learn languages easily. They _____ new words quickly.

6. I speak three _____ languages: English, Arabic, and French.

7. I think anyone can learn a language. What's your _____ ?

THINK VISUALLY

A. Look at the chart. Answer the questions.

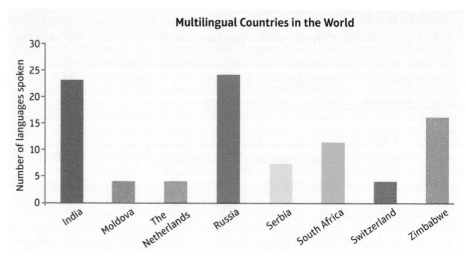

Multilingual Countries in the World

(Chart: Number of languages spoken)
- India: 23
- Moldova: 4
- The Netherlands: 4
- Russia: 24
- Serbia: 7
- South Africa: 11
- Switzerland: 4
- Zimbabwe: 16

1. What does the word *multilingual* mean?
   a. many countries
   b. many languages
   c. many people

2. What are the two parts of the word *multilingual*?
   a. mul-tilingual
   b. mu-litingual
   c. multi-lingual

3. Which country speaks the most languages?

   _____

4. How many languages does South Africa have?
   a. 4   b. 11   c. 23   d. 24

5. Which countries have the same number of languages?
   a. India and Russia
   b. Serbia and South Africa
   c. Moldova, The Netherlands, Switzerland

6. Which country has 23 languages?
   a. Russia
   b. India
   c. Zimbabwe

B. How many languages are spoken by the people in your country? How do people learn the languages?

GRAMMAR

USING *LIKE* + INFINITIVE VERB FORM

Read about the ways the people study languages. Complete the passages. Use a form of *like* + the infinitive of the verbs in the boxes. Use the example to help you.

~~practice~~	move	sit	walk

1. Jorge and Juan take the same French class.
   They *like to practice* speaking French together.
   They _____ for a long time. They both
   _____ while they study. So, every day
   after class, they _____ on campus.
   They speak French all the way to their dormitory!

draw	make	study	work

2. Parisa is a visual learner. She _____
   pictures of the new vocabulary words she learns in class.
   She also _____ charts to study the
   grammar. She _____ with anyone.
   She _____ alone.

play	study	take	use

3. Gabriela and Zhanetta _____ with
   books or paper. They _____ notes in
   class. They _____ their phones to study.
   For example, they _____ games or talk
   to other students in their class.

practice	travel	watch	write

4. Ivan _____ to different countries. He
   wants to go to Italy next. To study the language, he _____
   Italian movies. During the movie, he _____ the new vocabulary
   words in a notebook. Later, he _____ by saying the words
   out loud.

ASSIGNMENT

Think of ideas to help someone study a foreign language. Interview your classmates about how they like to learn. Then suggest language study activities that match their learning style.

PREPARE TO SPEAK

Work with a group. Think of fun or interesting activities to help someone study a language. Write your ideas in the chart under each way of studying.

Read	Write	Speak / Discuss
Listen	**Look at Pictures**	**Build or Make Things**
Move Around	**Study Alone**	**Study with Other People**

SPEAK

A. Go around the class. Talk to five classmates. Ask them how they like to learn. Then suggest one of your ideas from Prepare to Speak. Use the example to help you.

> A: Do you like to move around?
>
> B: Yes, I love to move around.
>
> A: OK. Listen to language podcasts at the gym.
>
> B: That's a good idea. Thanks!

B. Write down three classmates' ideas you liked. Share them with the class.

Student's Name	Idea

● Go to **MyEnglishLab** to complete grammar and vocabulary practices.

DEVELOP SOFT SKILLS

KNOWING YOUR PERSONAL LEARNING STYLE

Everyone has a different learning style. It's important to understand your personal learning style. This will help you build strong study skills and have success. When you understand how you learn, you will be able to learn better and faster. Then studying at university will be easier.

Glossary

advisor: someone who gives university students advice about classes, study skills, and careers

survey: a set of questions that you ask people in order to find out about their opinions or behavior

habit: something that you always do, often without thinking about it

out loud: in a way that people can hear

tap: hit your finger or foot against something gently

match: be like something else in size, shape, color, etc.

confident: feeling sure that you can do something well

concentrate: think very carefully about what you are doing

mix: a combination of different things or people

A. Zara has a meeting with her advisor to talk about study skills. The advisor asked Zara to complete a survey before their meeting. Look at Zara's answers on the learning styles survey on page 98. Answer the questions.

LEARNING STYLES SURVEY

Do you know your learning style? Are you an aural learner? A kinesthetic learner?
A visual learner? Answer the questions about how you like to learn.

Questions	Always 2 points	Sometimes 1 point	Never 0 points
1. Do you like to learn by listening to others?	✓		
2. Do you like to listen to music when you learn?	✓		
3. Do you like to say things out loud when you study?	✓		
4. Do you like to move around when you learn?		✓	
5. Do you like to learn by making or building things?			✓
6. Do you like to tap your foot or pen when you study?			✓
7. Do you like to study charts when you learn?			✓
8. Do you like to use colors to organize information?		✓	
9. Do you like quiet places when you study?		✓	

1. Write the learning style (visual / aural / kinesthetic)
   for each color.

   Green: _____

   Blue: _____

   Yellow: _____

2. Add up Zara's scores.

   Green: _____

   Blue: _____

   Yellow: _____

3. What is Zara's learning style?

   _____

🎧 **B. Listen to the first part of the conversation between Zara and her advisor.
Answer the questions.**

1. Where does Zara usually study?

   _____

2. What helps Zara concentrate?

   _____

3. What helps Zara remember?

   _____

C. Listen to the next part of the conversation between Zara and her advisor. Read the sentences. Circle *T* (true) or *F* (false). Correct the false statements.

T / F   1. Zara has one learning style.

_____

T / F   2. Zara likes to learn by listening.

_____

T / F   3. Zara likes to learn by seeing.

_____

T / F   4. All of Zara's study habits match her learning style.

_____

D. Work with a partner. Ask each other the questions about your study habits. Use the learning styles survey to find your personal learning style. Write your answers in the table below.

		Me	My Partner
1.	Where do you usually study?		
2.	What helps you concentrate?		
3.	What helps you remember?		
4.	What is your personal learning style?		

E. Do your study habits match your personal learning style? If not, what changes can you make to your study habits?

WHAT DID YOU LEARN?

Check (✓) the skills and vocabulary you learned. Circle the things you need to practice.

SKILLS

☐ I can listen for examples.

☐ I can identify and use collocations.

☐ I can express degrees of like and dislike.

☐ I know my personal learning style.

☐ I can use *like* + infinitive.

VOCABULARY

☐ best

☐ choose

☐ difficult

☐ discuss

☐ foreign

☐ helpful

☐ homework

☐ hope

☐ let

☐ need

☐ opinion

☐ pick up

☐ practice

☐ remember

☐ successful

☐ take notes

☐ way

⬆ Go to **MyEnglishLab** to complete a self-assessment.

⬆ Go to **MyEnglishLab** for a challenge listening about Genetics.

Business and Technology

Go to **MyEnglishLab** to see an introduction about **BUSINESS AND TECHNOLOGY**.

+6.04   +3.01
−1.35   −4.57
−7.02   −3.72
+9.03   +3.96
+14.28   +2.54
−11.32   −2.13
+9.45   +1.96
+8.35   +3.32

87   86.53   9   178.95
114   13.19   6   432.16
98   18.76   3   175.95
252   54.32   2   58.92
86   98.65   73   99.16
15   8.43   8   34.18
24   3.76   15   458.04
39   65.12   19   387.32
7   673.54

Chapter 5   In-Store or Online

CHAPTER PROFILE

Business is about making, selling, and buying things. People who study business think of ways to make money and have a successful job or career. Most businesses today use **technology**, like computers or robotics, to make and sell their products.

You will listen to

- a panel discussion about in-store and online shopping.

- people comparing stores and websites.

- a lecture about how e-commerce ideas can help local stores.

You will also

- give a short presentation comparing two stores or websites and their products

- give a presentation about products you bought.

OUTCOMES

- Understand words and phrases for comparing and contrasting
- State an opinion
- Express agreement and disagreement
- Understand and use comparative adjectives
- Understand and use large numbers
- Stay safe online

For more about **BUSINESS AND TECHNOLOGY**, see Chapter 6. See also [RW] **BUSINESS AND TECHNOLOGY**, Chapters 5 and 6.

GETTING STARTED

Read the list of items. Do you usually buy them in a store or on the Internet?
Write the items in the chart. Then compare with a partner. Use the sample
conversation below.

books	event tickets (concerts, sports)	movies
cars	food	music
cleaning supplies	gifts	personal care (shampoo, soap)
clothing	jewelry	shoes
electronics (computer, games)	medicine	travel / transportation (bus, train tickets)

In a Store	On the Internet

A: Where do you buy _____?

B: I buy _____ in a store / on the Internet. How about you?

🔊 Go to **MyEnglishLab** to complete a self-assessment.

LISTEN

SKILL: UNDERSTANDING WORDS AND PHRASES FOR COMPARING AND CONTRASTING

When you **compare** two or more items, you explain how they are the same. When you **contrast** two or more items, you explain how they are different. Speakers use special words or phrases when they are **comparing and contrasting**. When you know these words and phrases, you can understand when the speaker is explaining things that are the same or different.

Compare		Contrast	
all	like	although	only
also	same as	but	on the other hand
and	similar	different from	unlike
both	too	however	while

🎧 Listen to each speaker. Answer the questions.

Speaker 1

1. Is the speaker comparing or contrasting?

☐ comparing   ☐ contrasting

2. What is the gist?

_____

_____

3. What words helped you know?

_____

_____

Speaker 2

4. Is the speaker comparing or contrasting?

☐ comparing   ☐ contrasting

5. What is the gist?

_____

6. What words helped you know?

_____

Speaker 3

7. Is the speaker comparing or contrasting?

☐ comparing   ☐ contrasting

8. What is the gist?

_____

9. What words helped you know?

_____

REMEMBER

Write the words and phrases on the correct line.

all	both	like	similar
also	but	on the other hand	too
although	different from	only	unlike
and	however	same as	while

Compare: _____

_____

Contrast: _____

_____

VOCABULARY PREVIEW

A. Read the sentences. Look at the boldfaced words. Do you know what they mean? Share your ideas with a partner.

1. My friends and I like to buy gifts at **local** stores. Our town has some nice shops.

2. Those **companies** sell computers.

3. My parents **own** the ice-cream store in town.

4. That store has a lot of good **products**. I want to buy them all!

5. Martina likes to buy her clothes **online**. She uses her phone to buy them.

6. Do you **shop** at that store? I heard it has expensive things.

7. The number of stores in the city **increases** every year.

8. My grandparents like to talk to a **real** person in a store. Not someone on the computer.

9. I don't like to **wait,** so I shop in stores and not online.

10. The **service** at that store is excellent. The workers are very helpful.

B. Write the boldfaced words from Part A next to their definitions.

_____ 1. the help that workers give you in a store or restaurant

_____ 2. have something that belongs to you

_____ 3. things that people buy or sell

_____ 4. businesses; organizations (groups of people) that sell something

_____ 5. go to stores to buy things

_____ 6. true, not fake

_____ 7. not do something until someone comes or something happens

_____ 8. near where you live

_____ 9. connected to the Internet

_____ 10. becomes more in number, goes up

C. You will hear these sentences in the listening. Read them aloud with a partner. Do you remember the meanings of the boldfaced words?

1. **Local** businesses are the stores, shops, and **companies** near your home.

2. The people in your towns and cities **own** the local shops. Big international companies don't own them.

3. People go to these shops to buy **products** they need.

4. E-business means buying and selling things **online**.

5. In fact, it's almost the same. 51 percent of people like to **shop** in-store, and 49 percent of people like to shop online.

6. Online shopping sales **increase** every year.

7. Some **real** stores and companies closed because of e-commerce.

8. They don't want to **wait** for it to come to their house.

9. Another thing that is different is the **service**.

◑ Go to **MyEnglishLab** to complete a vocabulary practice.

PREDICT

Look at the pictures. Think about the speakers, the situation, and the topic. Then predict the words or phrases you will hear. Complete the chart.

E-business vs. Real Stores

Speakers	
Situation	
Topic	
Words and Phrases	

Glossary

sales: the amount of products a company sells

expert: a person with special knowledge or skill in a subject

shipping: delivering products to a place

24 / 7: open 24 hours a day, 7 days a week

LISTEN

A. Listen. Check (✓) if your predictions are correct or incorrect. For any that are incorrect, write the correct information.

	Correct	Incorrect	Correct Information
Speaker			
Situation			
Topic			
Words and Phrases			

B. Answer the questions about the gist of the discussion.

1. What is the gist (main topic) of the panel discussion?

   a. Online shopping is better than in-store shopping.

   b. Local stores are closing.

   c. There are different reasons that people shop in stores or online.

   d. People like to get their products quickly.

2. How are online shopping and in-store shopping the same?

    a. You don't pay for shipping.

    b. You can talk to someone about a product.

    c. The number of people who like to shop online and in-store is about the same.

    d. All of the above.

3. What topic did Mr. Bacas talk about?

    a. reasons people like to shop online

    b. reasons people like to shop in-store

    c. reasons people don't like big international stores

4. What topic did Ms. Kawamura talk about?

    a. reasons people like to shop online

    b. reasons people like to shop in-store

    c. reasons real companies close

🎧 **C. Listen to the excerpts from the discussion. Complete the missing information or choose the correct answers.**

SECTION 1

1. Local businesses are the _____ , _____ , and _____ in a city.

2. E-business, also called e-commerce, means buying and selling things _____ .

3. Who owns the local shops?

    a. big international companies

    b. people in your towns and cities

    c. the town

4. How many people shopped online in 2017?

    a. 16.6 billion

    b. 1.16 billion

    c. 1.66 billion

    d. 1.66 million

5. In what year will e-business increase to $4.48 trillion (US)?

    a. 2017

    b. 2020

    c. 2021

    d. 2023

SECTION 2

6. What happened to Toys "R" Us™ in 2017?

    a. It started online shopping.

    b. It closed.

    c. It changed its name.

7. Shopping in-store is still _____. In fact, it's almost the _____.

8. How many people like to shop online?

    a. 51%

    b. 39%

    c. 49%

9. People like to _____ and _____ the product before they buy it.

SECTION 3

10. Online shopping is _____ and _____.

11. It only takes a click on your _____ or _____ to shop.

12. When is online shopping open?

    a. 24/7

    b. 9 A.M. to 5 P.M.

    c. only on weekdays

LISTEN AGAIN

A. Listen again. Circle the reasons that Mr. Bacas says people like to shop in a store.

It's convenient.	They get the product now.
They get free shipping.	They like the experience of shopping.
They can ask questions to people in-store.	They like to touch the product.
They like to see other people shopping.	It's less expensive.
They get good service.	It takes too much time.
They don't like to pay online.	They like to see the product before they buy it.

B. Circle the reasons that Ms. Kawamura says people like to shop online.

It's easy.	It's a popular way to shop.
It's fun.	It's convenient.
They can shop anytime, anywhere.	They can touch the product.
You get free shipping.	They can compare prices quickly.
They don't like to wait in line.	They can ask questions about product.
They can shop 24/7.	They can buy products from all over the world.

C. Read the sentences. Circle *T* (True) or *F* (False). Correct the false statements.

T / F   1. Milos Bacas wrote a book called *E-commerce and Beyond.*

_____.

T / F   2. Online shopping sales increase every year.

_____.

T / F   3. In 2016, 1.66 billion people shopped online.

_____.

T / F   4. People say that online shopping will increase to 4.48 trillion dollars by the
            year 2021.

_____.

T / F   5. Fifty-one percent of people like to shop online and forty-nine percent of people
            like to shop in-store.

_____.

VOCABULARY REVIEW
Complete the sentences with words from the box.

company	local	own	real	shop
increases	online	products	service	wait

1. I like to buy _____ from that store. They work well and don't cost a lot
   of money.

2. Good _____ is important to me. I only go to stores that have workers to
   help me.

3. That store always has long lines. You have to _____ a long time to pay.

4. The _____ stores in my town are very expensive. I don't like to go there.

5. He works for a _____ that makes toys.

6. Online shopping _____ every year.

7. It is better to talk to a _____ person instead of a computer.

8. I always _____ at that store. The people there are very helpful.

9. My parents _____ a local toy store in town.

10. People who shop _____ use the Internet.

● **Go to MyEnglishLab for more listening practice.**

SPEAK

SKILL: STATING AN OPINION; EXPRESSING AGREEMENT AND DISAGREEMENT

There are many sides to a topic, and people have different opinions. To express your opinion, use these phrases:

I think …   In my opinion …

I believe …   I feel that …

When someone has the same or different opinion as you, you can express your agreement or disagreement. These words help you express your agreement or disagreement.

Agree		Disagree	
I agree.	That's right.	I don't agree.	I see your point, but …
Me, too.	Exactly!	I disagree.	I don't think so.

TIP

Disagreeing in a nice way

Disagreeing with someone can sometimes be difficult. To respect the people you're talking to, it is good to let them express their opinions, and then gently reply with your disagreement. Starting with the phrase *I see your point, but …* shows respect for other people.

Asking for opinions

When in a large group, it's always good to ask everyone's opinion. That way everyone feels included. Using the phrase *What do you think?* helps everyone get into the conversation.

Read the sample conversation. Underline all the words and phrases that express agreement and disagreement. Then practice the conversation with a partner.

A: I really like the new supermarket on Main Street. What do you think?

B: In my opinion, the old one was better.

A: Why do you say that?

B: Well, the old one had more choices.

A: I see your point, but the new one has better food.

B: I agree. This one has better fruit, and I love their cakes!

A: Me, too!

Write the phrases on the correct lines below.

I don't agree.	That's right!	I disagree.
I feel that …	Me, too.	I believe …
I don't think so.	I think …	Exactly!
I agree.	I see your point, but…	In my opinion …

Express your opinion _____

Agree: _____

Disagree: _____

What expression can you use to ask someone's opinion?

_____

Grammar for Speaking Understanding and using comparative adjectives

Adjectives are words that describe people, places, and things—for example, *big*, *small*, *good*, *bad*, *fast*, *slow*. When we compare two or more items, we use the **comparative** form of an adjective.

Here are the rules for forming **comparative adjectives**:

TYPE OF ADJECTIVE	RULES	EXAMPLE SENTENCES
One-syllable adjective (fast, big, small)	+ -er faster, smaller	Shopping online is **faster** than shopping in a store.
Two-syllable adjectives ending in y (easy, busy)	+ -ier easier, busier	Shopping online is **easier** than going to a store.
Two-syllable adjectives (helpful, famous)	+ more more helpful, more famous	Staff at local stores are **more helpful** than online stores.
Three- or more syllable adjectives (difficult, expensive)	+ more more difficult more expensive	Shopping in a store is **more difficult** than shopping online.
Irregular adjectives (good, bad, far)	good – better bad – worse far – farther	Shopping in local stores is much **better** than shopping online.

GRAMMAR NOTE

Some one-syllable adjectives use *more*: *fun = more fun*; *real = more real*.

If the speakers know the topic, you do not need to use a complete sentence.

    A: Do you like to shop online or in a store?

    B: I like to shop online.

    A: Why?

    B: Because it is faster and easier (than shopping online).

    A: But isn't shopping online more expensive?

    B: No, it's less expensive. I can find some good deals!

A. Complete the sentences with the comparative form of the adjective.

1. The ABC Toy store is _____ than our local toy store. (large)

2. The fruit at local grocery stores is _____ than the fruit online. (healthy)

3. I feel _____ _____ shopping online. (comfortable)

4. People in local stores are _____ _____ than people in online stores. (hardworking)

5. In my opinion, it is _____ to shop online. (easy)

6. We like to shop at that book store. It is _____ than the big book store on Main Street. (quiet)

7. Going to local stores is _____ _____ than shopping online. (fun)

8. The selection is _____ in local stores. (small)

9. You have to wait a long time in that store. This store has a _____ wait time. (short)

10. I like this store _____ than that store. It has _____ clothes. (good); (nice)

GRAMMAR NOTE

Comparatives with less: *Less + adjective* is used when the person or thing is less (not as much). Regular comparatives are used more often. For example: *Shopping online is less exciting than going to a store. But it's also less expensive.*

B. Complete the sentences with a comparative adjective. Then circle the store you like best.

1. The workers at Super Shoes are hardworking, but the workers at Feet First are
   _____ . (helpful)

   a. Super Shoes   b. Feet First

2. The products in Super Shoes are less expensive. However, the products in Feet First are
   _____ . (nice)

   a. Super Shoes   b. Feet First

3. Super Shoes has good products. On the other hand, Feet First has _____
   service. (good)

   a. Super Shoes   b. Feet First

4. Super Shoes has great prices; while Feet First has _____ products. (beautiful)

   a. Super Shoes   b. Feet First

5. Super Shoes has nice products, but Feet First has _____ service. (fast)

   a. Super Shoes   b. Feet First

C. Think of two places (stores, restaurants, hotels). Write three sentences to contrast them (like the sentences in Part B). Use comparative adjectives and different phrases for contrasting.

_____ .

_____ .

_____ .

D. Read your sentences to five classmates. Ask them to choose between the two places. Follow the sample conversation.

A: Store A has great prices, but Store B has more beautiful products. Which store do you want to go to?

B: In my opinion, beautiful products are more important than better prices. I choose Store B.

E. For each adjective, check (✓) *Shopping in a Store* or *Shopping Online*. Then tell your partner your opinion using a comparative adjective. Follow the example below.

	Shopping in a Store	Shopping Online
expensive		
convenient		
fast		
helpful staff		
easy		
fun		
good service		
bad		

A: I think shopping in a store is more expensive.

B: I don't agree. Shopping online is more expensive. You have to pay for shipping.

↻ Go to **MyEnglishLab** for more grammar practice.

COMPARE AND CONTRAST TWO STORES OR WEBSITES

STEP 1: LISTEN BEFORE YOU SPEAK

A. Look at the pictures. Think about the speakers, the situation, and the topic. Then predict the words and phrases you will hear. Complete the chart.

Speakers	
Situation	
Topic	
Words and Phrases	

B. Read the words and definitions. You will hear these words in the listening.

> **Glossary**
>
> staff: a group of people who work together at a store or company
> workers: people who work
> website: a program on a computer that gives information about a product or subject
> goods: things like food or clothes you can buy or sell
> dishes: things we eat on and drink from (plate, bowl, cup)
> bedding: the covers or blankets you put on your bed to keep you warm
> customer: a person who buys things in a store or online
> ready: prepared or able to do something
> fresh: in good condition because it was picked a short time ago

C. Listen to the first speaker. Complete the tasks.

1. The speaker is comparing and contrasting _____ .

   a. online stores vs. local businesses   c. different kinds of businesses

   b. product prices   d. two local stores

2. Which store does the speaker like better?

   a. Clothing Corner   b. The Clothes Closet

3. Write three things the speaker says about Clothing Corner and three things the speaker says about The Clothes Closet.

Clothing Corner	The Clothes Closet

4. Which clothing store do you think is better? Check (✔) your choice. Then compare with a partner. Explain why.

   ☐ Clothing Corner   ☐ The Clothes Closet

D. Listen to the second speaker. Complete the tasks.

1. The speaker is comparing and contrasting _____ .

   a. an online store and a local store   c. two homes

   b. two websites   d. prices online

2. Which website does the speaker like better?

   a. Homestore.com

   b. YourHome.com

3. Write three things the speaker says about Homestore.com and three things the speaker says about YourHome.com

	Homestore.com	YourHome.com
1.	_____	_____
2.	_____	_____
3.	_____	_____

4. Which website do you think is better? Check (✓) your choice. Then compare with a partner. Explain why.

☐ Homestore.com   ☐ YourHome.com

STEP 2: PREPARE TO SPEAK

A. You are going to compare two stores or websites. Read the audio scripts from Step 1. Follow these instructions:

1. Underline the phrases for comparing and contrasting.

2. Circle the words and phrases for giving opinions and agreeing / disagreeing.

3. Draw a box around the comparative adjectives.

SPEAKER 1

There are two clothing stores in town. One is called Clothing Corner, and the other is The Clothes Closet. In my opinion, Clothing Corner is much better than The Clothes Closet. First, Clothing Corner is bigger. It also has more beautiful products. The staff are more helpful and more hardworking than the workers at The Clothes Closet. The clothes at Clothing Corner are also more comfortable. They feel better. There are some good things about The Clothes Closet, however. The clothing there is less expensive than at Clothing Corner. The clothes at Clothing Corner are more fun, but, on the other hand, the clothes at The Clothes Closet are cooler. However, all in all, in my opinion, Clothing Corner is a much nicer store.

SPEAKER 2

There are two websites that I really like. One is called Homestore.com, and the other is called YourHome.com. They both sell home products and goods, like dishes, bedding, furniture, and food. In my opinion, they are both good, but for different reasons. Homestore.com has a very good website, but YourHome.com has better customer service. When I have a question about something, someone on YourHome.com is ready to talk to me. In my opinion, the products on YourHome.com are very nice, but, on the other hand, they are more expensive than the products on Homestore.com. The furniture on Homestore.com is more comfortable; however, the furniture at YourHome.com is more interesting. They have different types of furniture. The food on Homestore.com is very good; however, the food on YourHome.com is healthier. They buy their food from local businesses, so the food is fresher. I like both websites, but I usually go to YourHome.com first.

B. Think of two places (shops, restaurants, hotels) or websites. How are they the same or different? Which one do you like better? Make notes in the chart below to compare and contrast them. Use adjectives from the box or think of your own.

beautiful	far	helpful	nice	short	ugly
boring	fun	interesting	normal	shy	wonderful
comfortable	great	large	quiet	small	
cool	hardworking	lazy	real	tall	
dirty	healthy	loud	serious	terrible	

Place / Website A	Place / Website B
Name:	Name:

C. Use the sentence starters below for your presentation:

In my opinion …   I believe …

I think …   Place A is _____ than Place B.

STEP 3: SPEAK

Practice your presentation.

1. Look up when you say your lines.

2. Show pictures of the two places, if possible.

3. Give your presentation to the class.

STEP 4: PEER FEEDBACK

Write the names of three classmates in the first column. Listen to their presentations. Write the names of the places, which place they like better, and 1–2 reasons for their opinions. Follow the example.

Classmates' Names	Places	Which Place Person Likes Better	Reasons
Carla	Clothing Corner and The Clothes Closet	Clothing Corner	1. Bigger 2. More helpful staff

BUILDING VOCABULARY

UNDERSTANDING AND USING LARGE NUMBERS

When we talk about business, we often need to use large numbers. Large numbers are useful when we compare companies, numbers of products, customers, sales, or amounts of money.

🔊 A. Read the sentences. Do you know how to say the boldfaced numbers? Listen and circle the correct numbers. Then practice saying the sentences with a partner.

1. In 2018, there were $**123,000,000,000** in online sales in the United States.

   a. one hundred twenty-three billion   b. one hundred twenty-three million

2. By 2019, there will be **224,000,000** digital shoppers in the United States.

   a. two hundred twenty-four thousand   b. two hundred twenty-four million

3. Mobile e-commerce, shopping by phone, was over $**3,000,000,000,000** dollars in 2017.

   a. three hundred thousand   b. three trillion

4. There are **245,000** companies with web sales in the United States.

   a. two hundred forty-five thousand   b. two hundred forty-five hundred

5. In 2018, there were almost **2,000,000,000** online shoppers around the world.

   a. two million   b. two billion

6. By 2021, e-commerce sales will be over $**4,000,000,000,000**.

   a. forty trillion   b. four trillion

B. Write the matching numbers and phrases in the chart. Then check your answers with a partner.

1,000,000,000   100,000   one million   one hundred   1,000   ten thousand   one trillion

Numbers	Phrases
100	
	one thousand
10,000	
	one hundred thousand
1,000,000	
	one billion
1,000,000,000,000	

C. Read the sentences. Write the correct number (in words) below each sentence. Listen and check your answers. Then practice reading the sentences aloud to a partner.

1. E-business sales in the United States is a ($353,000,000,000) business.

   $_____

2. By 2019, there may be (224,000,000) online shoppers in the United States.

   _____

3. In 2017, e-commerce was around ($23,000,000,000,000) in sales around the world.

   $_____

4. On average, people in the United States spend ($1,804) online every year.

   $_____

5. New businesses make between ($34,392) and ($105,757) per year.

   between $ _____ and $_____

◯ Go to **MyEnglishLab** to complete a vocabulary practice.

APPLY YOUR SKILLS

In this chapter, you listened to a class discussion about the reasons that people shop online or in local stores. You also compared two places or websites. In Apply Your Skills, you will listen to a lecture about how e-commerce can help local businesses. Then you will give a short presentation on a product you bought.

VOCABULARY PREVIEW

A. Read the sentences. Look at the boldfaced words and phrases. Do you know what they mean? Share your ideas with a partner.

1. The Internet is used **worldwide**.

2. It is difficult for local stores to **compete** with e-commerce.

3. Some local stores don't do well and **fail**.

4. The new **owners** of that store try many things to help their business.

5. That store has many **workers**. They are all very helpful.

6. Abdul and Samira **continue** the business that their grandparents started.

7. Our **plan** is to use the Internet to increase our business.

8. I like to see the product **in person**. I like to feel it and look at it.

9. The Internet can help **grow** your company.

B. Write the boldfaced words and phrases from Part A next to their definitions.

_____ 1. people who do a job

_____ 2. not do well at something, not be successful

_____ 3. decision to do something

_____ 4. people who own / have something

_____ 5. everywhere in the world; within the world

_____ 6. increase in size or amount

_____ 7. when you are in a place, not by phone, computer or on the Internet

_____ 8. try to win

_____ 9. keep happening or doing something without stopping

Go to **MyEnglishLab** to complete a vocabulary practice.

PREDICT

Look at the pictures. Think about the speaker, the situation, and the topic. Then predict the words and phrases you will hear. Complete the chart.

Speaker	
Situation	
Topic	
Words and Phrases	

Glossary

decrease: become less or smaller

go out of business: close a business forever

reservation: an arrangement with a hotel or restaurant to hold a room or a table for you

review: a written opinion about a person's experience with a business or company

LISTEN

🔊 **A. Listen. Were your predictions correct? Which ones? Tell a partner.**

My prediction was correct / incorrect about …

B. Circle the gist of the lecture.

a. People like online stores better than local stores.

b. Local stores are more expensive than online stores.

c. Local stores can use the Internet to increase business.

🔊 **C. Listen to the excerpts from the lecture. Choose the correct answer.**

SECTION 1

1. According to the lecture, how many people use the Internet?

   a. 6.3 billion   b. 3.6 billion   c. 30.6 billion

2. E-commerce is a _____ business.

   a. million-dollar   b. billion-dollar   c. trillion-dollar

3. Research shows that 90 percent of shopping happens _____ .

   a. online   b. in stores   c. with friends

SECTION 2

4. E-businesses don't need _____ .

   a. a website   b. a building   c. an owner

5. It is _____ expensive to have an e-business.

   a. less   b. more

6. E-business is open 24 / 7, 365 days a year, but a local store is only open about _____ a day.

   a. 18 hours   b. 8–10 hours   c. 2–10 hours

7. What does 24 / 7 mean?

   a. 24 days, 7 weeks a year   b. 24 hours, 7 days a week   c. from 12:00 to 7:00

SECTION 3

8. Store owners that change their _____ do well.

   a. name   b. plan   c. products

9. A good review is _____ .

   a. 1–2 stars   b. 3–4 stars   c. 4–5 stars

10. A review on a website can _____ a business.

   a. help   b. hurt   c. help or hurt

LISTEN AGAIN

A. Listen again. Write three things the teacher says about e-businesses and local stores.

	E-Business	Local Store
1.		
2.		
3.		

B. Work in a group. Discuss the questions.

1. How can stores use the Internet to grow their business?

2. Check (✔) all the ways you like to shop. Then discuss with your group.

   ☐ Go to a store's website and look at their products. Then go and see the product in person.

   ☐ Read customer reviews.

   ☐ Go to a store's Facebook, Twitter, or Instagram page (or another social media site).

3. Do you write reviews for online or local stores? Tell about a store you wrote a comment about. How many stars did you give?

VOCABULARY REVIEW

Complete the sentences with words and phrases from the box.

compete	fail	in person	plan	worldwide
continue	grow	owner	workers	

1. The Internet can help _____ your business.

2. The _____ of that store is smart. She also sells her products online.

3. I like to talk to a worker _____ about the product. I get more information about the product.

4. Many people like to shop online, but my grandparents don't. They _____ to shop in the local stores.

5. There are many Internet users _____.

6. Local stores can _____ with online stores when they get a website.

7. It is important to have good _____ in your store. They can help the customers with questions.

8. I don't like to see local stores _____. It's sad to see them close.

9. Her _____ is to open a local store and get a website.

THINK VISUALLY

Look at the chart and answer the questions.

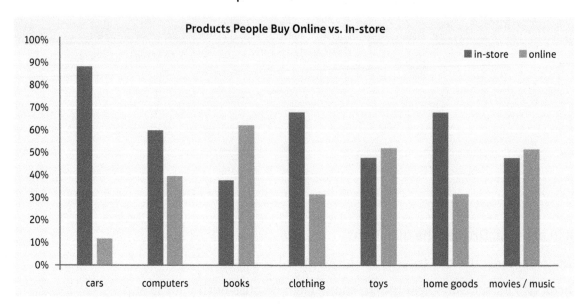

Products People Buy Online vs. In-store

in-store ■ online ■

cars   computers   books   clothing   toys   home goods   movies / music

1. Do shoppers prefer online or in-store shopping with these products? Circle the answers.

   Cars: Online   In-store

   Books: Online   In-store

   Home goods: Online   In-store

   Movies / Music: Online   In-store

2. What percentage of people like to buy their computers online?

   a. 60%   b. 40%   c. 50%

3. Which product has the least amount of people who buy it online?

   a. books   b. home goods   c. cars

4. Which products have the same percentages?

   a. computers and books   b. movies / music and toys

5. Look at the percentages. Write a sentence to compare or contrast them to the way you like to shop. _____

GRAMMAR

USING AND UNDERSTANDING COMPARATIVE ADJECTIVES

Write the comparative form of the adjectives in the box. Then choose comparatives to complete the conversations below. Practice the conversations with a partner.

convenient _____	great _____	interesting _____
cool _____	hardworking _____	nice _____
fast _____	helpful _____	quiet _____

1. A: Do you like to shop online or in a local store?

   B: I like to shop _____ because it is _____ .

2. A: Do you like to talk to staff in a store or email your questions online?

   B: I like to _____ because they are / it is _____.

3. A: What is better about shopping online?

   B: It is _____ and _____ than shopping in a store.

4. A: What is better about shopping in a local store?

   B: It is _____ and _____ than shopping online.

ASSIGNMENT

Give a review of a recent shopping experience.

PREPARE TO SPEAK

A. Think of a product or service that you buy or use often. Choose an idea from the list or add your own.

Products	Services
book	restaurant
clothes	mechanic (to fix a car)
shoes	hair salon (haircut, etc.)
school products (paper, pens, pencils, etc.)	My idea: _____
computer	
furniture	
car	
My idea: _____	

B. Complete the feedback form for your product or service.

Product / Service Feedback	
Where do you buy it? (in-store / online / both)	Name of store / business / restaurant: _____ In-store / online / both: _____
Did you do research (compare prices, learn about product) before buying it?	☐ Yes ☐ No If you checked *Yes*, how did you research? Circle or write. looked at website / asked friends / used social media Another way: _____
Are you happy with the product? Give a review. Color the number of stars. (5 is best.)	Product / Service: ☆☆☆☆☆ Price: ☆☆☆☆☆
Do you recommend this product / service / business to other people? Why or why not?	Yes / No _____ Why / Why not? _____

C. Practice your review. Show a picture or bring the product to class and show your classmates. Use the examples to help you.

I got / bought a ....

I went to ....

I got it online. The website is ....

I got it at a store. The store is ....

I gave the product / service ... stars.

I gave the price ... stars.

I am (not) happy / not happy with the product because ....

I am happy / unhappy with the store because ....

In my opinion, ...

I recommend / don't recommend this product / service because ....

SPEAK

A. Give your review to the class.

B. Listen to your group members' presentations and complete the chart.

Classmates' Names	Product / Service	Where They Got It (Online / In-Store)	Review—How Many Stars?
			Product / Service: Price:
			Product / Service: Price:
			Product / Service: Price:
			Product / Service: Price:
			Product / Service: Price:
			Product / Service: Price:

⊙ Go to **MyEnglishLab** to complete grammar and vocabulary practices.

DEVELOP SOFT SKILLS

STAYING SAFE ONLINE

Most of us use the Internet almost every day. We buy goods and services, make reservations, shop, stay in touch with friends, and even take university classes online. Usually companies have ways to keep your personal information private—so no one else can see it. But it isn't always 100 percent safe. Some bad people steal and use other people's information, for example, credit card numbers. You need to know how to keep your information safe.

> **Glossary**
>
> research: careful study, especially to find out new facts about something
>
> conditions: an agreement between you and a company, which says what a company can do with your information, and what you must do for the company
>
> accept: take something that is offered to you
>
> discover: learn about something for the first time
>
> attention: special care or interest that you give to someone or something

A. Work with a partner or small group. Complete the tasks.

1. What do you do online? Check (✓) the activities. Then compare with a partner or classmate.

☐ banking	☐ make reservations	☐ take lessons or classes
☐ do research	☐ read blogs or news	☐ use social media
☐ edit photos or videos	☐ shop	☐ watch TV or movies

2. How do you stay safe online? Circle your ideas. Then compare and discuss with a partner.

create a strong password	don't shop online	keep social media private (only close friends)
don't post photos	don't use public devices	read the conditions carefully

3. What are some problems that can happen with your online information? Work with a partner and list as many as you can. Use the photos to help you.

B. Listen to the first part of a lecture about staying safe online. Read the sentences. Circle True (*T*) or False (*F*). Correct the false statements.

T / F   1. Shopping in a store is safer than shopping online.

_____

T / F   2. People don't need to worry about putting personal information online.

_____

T / F   3. Most people read the conditions before they click "yes."

_____

T / F   4. Researchers made a website to find out how many people read the conditions.

_____

T / F   5. In the research study, 543 people did not read the conditions.

_____

C. Listen to the rest of the lecture. Answer the questions.

1. What information do social media sites get?

_____

2. What can someone do if they get your password?

_____

3. Which password is the best?
   a. 12345   b. MuMMer   c. p@ssw0rd98

4. What advice does the speaker give for staying safe online?

_____

_____

_____

_____

_____

D. Think of other ways you can stay safe online. Then discuss your ideas with a group. Make a list of tips to share with the class.

WHAT DID YOU LEARN?

Check (✓) the skills and vocabulary you learned. Circle the things you need to practice.

SKILLS

☐ I can understand words and phrases for comparing and contrasting.

☐ I can state an opinion.

☐ I can express agreement and disagreement.

☐ I can understand and use comparative adjectives.

☐ I can understand and use large numbers.

☐ I can stay safe online.

VOCABULARY

☐ bedding	☐ fail	☐ local	☐ staff
☐ billion	☐ fresh	☐ million	☐ ten thousand
☐ company	☐ goods	☐ owner	☐ thousand
☐ compare	☐ grow	☐ plan	☐ trillion
☐ compete	☐ hundred	☐ product	☐ wait
☐ continue	☐ hundred thousand	☐ ready	☐ website
☐ customer	☐ increase	☐ real	☐ worker
☐ dishes	☐ in-person	☐ service	☐ worldwide

◐ Go to **MyEnglishLab** to complete a self-assessment.

<table>
<tr><td>Chapter 6</td><td></td></tr>
</table>

Chapter 6   Changing with the Times

CHAPTER PROFILE

The business world is always changing. Many companies now use faster, less expensive ways to make products, for example, 3-D printing and robotics. This chapter is about how technology is changing the business world and people's jobs.

You will listen to

- a sales presentation about 3-D printing.

- a talk about how to start a business.

- a presentation about how to find a job.

You will also

- give instructions for an activity or a process.

- give instructions for a skill.

OUTCOMES

- Listen for instructions and steps
- Ask for and give instructions
- Understand and use imperatives
- Understand and use job-search vocabulary
- Use graphic organizers to study vocabulary

For more about **BUSINESS AND TECHNOLOGY**, see Chapter 5. See also RW **BUSINESS AND TECHNOLOGY**, Chapters 5 and 6.

GETTING STARTED

A. Look at the pictures. How do businesses use technology? Read the statements. Are they true about robots, humans, or both? Write *R* (robots), *H* (humans), or *B* (both).

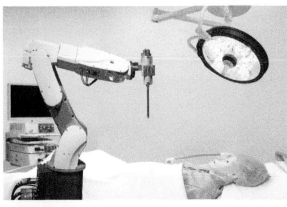
Healthcare

Manufacturing

Banking

Architectural Design

_____ 1. They do not enjoy boring jobs.

_____ 2. They take vacations.

_____ 3. They do not get sick.

_____ 4. They can work very fast for long hours.

_____ 5. They can do dangerous work.

_____ 6. They need a lot of training.

_____ 7. They sometimes need to take a break.

_____ 8. They sometimes make mistakes.

_____ 9. They are creative about solving problems.

_____ 10. They cost companies money.

_____ 11. They sometimes break and need repairs.

_____ 12. They bring new ideas to the company.

B. Work with a partner. Write your own statements about robots and humans in business. Try to think of one "pro" (good thing) and one "con" (bad thing) about each. Then share your statements with the class.

ROBOTS

Pro	Con

HUMANS

Pro	Con

⬆ Go to **MyEnglishLab** to complete a self-assessment.

LISTEN

SKILL: LISTENING FOR INSTRUCTIONS AND STEPS

Instructions are a list of steps in a sequence (in order). Speakers use special signal words to introduce each new step. When you listen to a list of instructions, these words will help you identify and follow the steps. Look at the examples.

First, …	Next, …
To begin, …	After, …
Second, …	Later, …
Third, …	Finally, …
Then …	Last, …

PRONUNCIATION NOTE

🔊 **Listen and repeat the sentences.**

First, press the power button.

Next, enter the information on the computer.

Then wait until the green light turns on.

Last, click "Start."

Speakers usually stress the sequence word in a sentence. They also often pause after the sequence word.

To begin | write your answers.

A. Listen to the instructions. Complete the tasks.

1. What are the instructions for?

   a. headphones   b. a cell phone

2. Number the instructions in order.

   _____ a. Click the "play" button on the computer.

   _____ b. Wait for the blue light to come on.

   _____ c. Find the on / off button on the side.

   _____ d. Push the button for five seconds.

   _____ e. Raise your hand if you need help.

   _____ f. Connect them to the computer.

B. Listen to the instructions. Complete the tasks.

1. What are the instructions for?

   a. a camera   b. a copy machine

2. Number the instructions in order.

   _____ a. Type the number of copies you want to make.

   _____ b. Put your original document in the top tray.

   _____ c. Take your document off the top tray.

   _____ d. Wait for the green light.

   _____ e. Pick up your copies on the side.

   _____ f. Turn the machine on.

   _____ g. Be sure there is paper in the paper drawer.

   _____ h. Press the "start" button.

REMEMBER

Complete the sentences.

Instructions are usually a list of several steps in a _____.

Speakers use special signal words to introduce each new _____.

When you listen to a list of _____, these words will help you identify and follow the steps.

Write the signal words on the correct lines.

after	finally	first	last	later	next	second	then	third	to begin

Words That Come in the Beginning of the Instructions _____

Words That Come in the Middle of the Instructions _____

Words That Come at the End of the Instructions _____

VOCABULARY PREVIEW

A. Read the sentences. Look at the boldfaced words and phrases. Do you know what they mean? Share your ideas with a partner.

1. Make sure you put the paper in the **correct** place.
2. This computer is **like** the computer at my house.
3. 3-D printers can make many kinds of **objects**.
4. I don't think this machine **works**. I need to fix it.
5. Martin knows how to use the machine. He can teach us the **steps**.
6. I didn't hear the first step of the instructions. Can you **begin** again, please?
7. What is the **size** of the machine?
8. Companies **save money** by using 3-D printers.
9. Please **cut** the paper into two pieces.
10. I **save time** by shopping online.

B. Write the boldfaced words and phrases from Part A next to their definitions.

_____ 1. keep money, to not spend money

_____ 2. divide or open something with a knife or scissors

_____ 3. right, with no mistakes

_____ 4. operates correctly

_____ 5. use less time

_____ 6. start

_____ 7. similar, almost the same

_____ 8. how big or small something or someone is

_____ 9. things

_____ 10. actions in a series of instructions

C. You will hear these sentences in the listening. Read them aloud with a partner. Do you remember the meanings of the boldfaced words and phrases?

1. Is that right? Yes, that's **correct**.

2. Are they **like** regular printers?

3. A 3-D printer prints three-dimensional **objects**.

4. How does the machine **work**?

5. I can explain the **steps**.

6. Well, we **begin** on the computer.

7. Third, get the printer ready for the object **size**.

8. Well, it **saves money**.

9. Companies don't **cut** the materials.

10. 3-D printers **save time**, too.

🔊 Go to **MyEnglishLab** to complete a vocabulary practice.

PREDICT

Look at the pictures. Think about the speakers, the situation, and the topic. Then predict the words and phrases you will hear. Complete the chart.

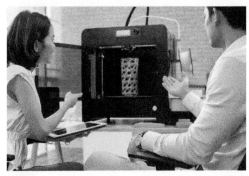
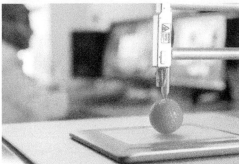

Speaker	
Situation	
Topic	
Words and Phrases	

LISTEN

A. Look at the photos and read the words. You will hear these words in the conversation.

layers

plastic

metal

concrete

ceramic

B. Listen. Check (✓) if your predictions are correct or incorrect. For any that are incorrect, write the correct information.

	Correct	Incorrect	Correct Information
Speaker			
Situation			
Topic			
Words and Phrases			

C. Check (✓) the topics the speakers talked about in the conversation.

☐ 1. The difference between regular printers and 3-D printers

☐ 2. How 3-D printing works

☐ 3. Different types of 3-D printers

☐ 4. Companies that make 3-D printers

☐ 5. Steps to use a 3-D printer

☐ 6. Materials used for 3-D printing

☐ 7. How companies save money and time with 3-D printers

D. Listen to the excerpts from the sales presentation. Choose the correct answers.

SECTION 1

1. Who is Luis Rivera?

   a. a worker at ABC Toys
   b. a worker at 3-D Plus Printers
   c. the owner of ABC Toys

2. Who is Helga Sanderson?

   a. a worker at ABC Toys
   b. a worker at 3-D Plus Printers
   c. the owner of ABC Toys

3. Luis Rivera wants to _____.

   a. learn how to use a 3-D printer

   b. sell a 3-D printer to Helga

   c. get a job at ABC Toys

4. How does a 3-D printer work?

   a. The printer prints a design from a computer.

   b. The printer cuts the material to form an object.

   c. The printer prints a picture. Then workers make the object.

SECTION 2

5. What object does Luis show how to make on the 3-D printer?

   a. a paper cup
   b. a toy animal
   c. a pencil

6. What kind of material can the 3-D printer use? Circle all that Luis talks about.

   a. plastic
   b. paper
   c. metal
   d. concrete
   e. wood
   f. ceramic

SECTION 3

7. 3-D printers are good for _____.

   a. the environment, business, and scientists

   b. workers, sales people, and companies

   c. companies, customers, and the environment

8. How are 3-D printers good for companies?

   a. They are not expensive.

   b. They save money and time.

   c. They are modern.

9. With 3-D printers, a customer _____.

   a. can get what he or she wants
   b. is always correct
   c. pays less money

LISTEN AGAIN

A. Listen again. Number the 3-D printer instructions in the correct order.

_____ 1. Turn the printer on and start printing.

_____ 2. Choose the object you want to make.

_____ 3. Put the material in the printer.

_____ 4. Enter the design code on the computer.

_____ 5. Take the object off the printer.

_____ 6. Get the printer ready for the object size.

B. Read the sentences. Circle _T_ (true) or _F_ (false). Correct the false statements.

T / F   1. ABC Toys has a 3-D printer.

_____

T / F   2. Helga Sanderson knows a lot about 3-D printers.

_____

T / F   3. 3-D printing begins on a computer.

_____

T / F   4. Many companies use 3-D printers.

_____

T / F   5. ABC Toys makes plastic toys.

_____

T / F   6. Customers like 3-D printing because they get what they want.

_____

T / F   7. 3-D printers make plastic, metal, concrete, and ceramic objects.

_____

T / F   8. 3-D printers are bad for the environment.

_____

C. Check (✓) the good things about 3-D printers that Luis talks about.

☐ 1. Companies save money.

☐ 2. Companies only make the number of products they need.

☐ 3. Companies can show customers a model of the product.

☐ 4. There is no waste.

☐ 5. The machines do not make mistakes.

☐ 6. Companies save time.

☐ 7. Customers can get what they want.

D. What are other examples of technology in business? Work in a small group. Write at least one example for each category. Then share your ideas with the class.

Technology that …

helps businesses save time: _____

helps companies save money: _____

is good for the environment: _____

helps customers get what they want: _____

VOCABULARY REVIEW

Complete the sentences with words from the box.

begin	cut	object	save time	step
correct	like	save money	size	work

1. Can I use your computer? My computer doesn't _____ .

2. I want to buy a 3-D printer. They are expensive. I need to _____ .

3. What _____ is the computer screen? I want to get a big screen.

4. 3-D printers are not _____ normal printers. They can print objects.

5. I made a mistake. Can I _____ again?

6. It is difficult to _____ this plastic. It's very thick.

7. 3-D printers _____ for companies. They can make their products faster.

8. What is the _____ way to use this machine?

9. The last _____ is to turn off the machine.

10. 3-D printers make any type of _____ .

🔊 Go to **MyEnglishLab** for more listening practice.

SPEAK

SKILL: ASKING FOR AND GIVING INSTRUCTIONS

When you don't know how to do something, it's important to know how to ask for instructions. When we give instructions, we use sequence words to introduce each step. These words help order the instructions. Sequence words help people know what to do first, next, and last.

A. Read the questions for asking for instruction and the sequence words for giving instructions.

Asking for Instructions	Giving Instructions
How do I / you …?	Before you begin, …
Can you tell me how to …?	First, …
What is the best way to …?	Second, …
What is the first step?	Then …
What is the next step?	Next, …
What do I do next?	After that, …
	Later, …
	Last, …
	Finally, …

B. Read the conversation. Underline all the expressions that relate to asking for and giving instructions. Then practice the conversation with a partner.

A: Do you know about cell phone apps?

B: Yes. I have some apps on my phone.

A: Can you tell me how to use this health app?

B: Oh, sure. I have the same app!

A: Great. How do I start?

B: Before you begin, you have to make your account.

A: OK. What is the first step?

B: First, you need to click on "Profile" and type in your information.

A: OK, what do I do next?

B: After that, choose the area you want to focus on. For example, eating healthy, exercising more, or managing stress.

A: OK. I want to exercise more.

B: Select the exercise icon. Then touch "save changes." Finally, watch your phone for updates.

A: Thank you so much!

C. Work with a partner. Choose an app on your cell phone. Take turns asking for and giving instructions for how to use each app. Use the examples to help you.

A: What's this app?

B: It's a weather app.

A: Can you tell me how to use it?

B: Sure. First, you …

Helpful Words

choose	select
click	swipe
press	tab
screen	touch

REMEMBER

Write three questions we can use to ask for instructions.

_____?

_____?

_____?

Grammar for Speaking Understanding and using imperatives

We use the imperative form of a verb to give instructions. To make the imperative, use the infinitive of the verb without the *to*.

AFFIRMATIVE	NEGATIVE
Push the button.	Do not / Don't push the button.
Cut the paper.	Do not / Don't cut the paper.

GRAMMAR NOTE

To be more polite or formal, use the word *please* before the imperative. *Please cut the paper.*

A. Complete the conversations with the imperative form of the verbs from the box.

to check	to hold	to look	not to touch	to press	to wait

1. A: My computer doesn't work. Can you help me?

   B: Sure. First, _____ the power cord. Is the computer plugged in?

   A: Yes, it is.

   B: OK. Next, _____ the power button. _____ it down for ten seconds.

   A: It works! _____! Do you see that light? What button do I press next?

   B: _____ anything. Just _____ for the computer to come on.

to choose	to click	to enter	to look	to type	to wait

2. A: I want to buy my father a gift online, but I don't know how to use this website. Can you tell me?

   B: Sure. Do you know what you want to buy?

   A: Yes. I want to get this hat.

   B: OK. First, _____ the color and size you want.

   A: Medium, red. OK.

   B: Then _____ on the picture of the medium red hat. Next, in the price box, _____ the price you want to pay.

   A: OK. What do I do next?

   B: Just _____ for the seller to accept your price.

   A: Oh, _____! It says accepted!

   B: Great! Last, _____ your address and your credit card information.

B. Work with a partner. Each partner chooses Task A or Task B. Look at the pictures for the instructions for each task. Use the pictures and your own ideas to write instructions and then tell your partner how to do the task. Remember to use the imperative form.

TASK A: INSTRUCTIONS FOR RIDE-SHARING SERVICE

1. _____ .

2. _____ .

3. _____ .

4. _____ .

5. _____ .

6. _____ .

TASK B: INSTRUCTIONS FOR GETTING A JOB

1. _____.
2. _____.
3. _____.
4. _____.
5. _____.

Go to **MyEnglishLab** for more grammar practice.

GIVE INSTRUCTIONS FOR AN ACTIVITY OR A PROCESS

STEP 1: LISTEN BEFORE YOU SPEAK

A. Look at the picture. Think about the speaker, the situation, and the topic. Then predict the words and phrases you will hear. Complete the chart.

Speaker	
Situation	
Topic	
Words and Phrases	

B. Read the words and definitions. You will hear these words in the conversation.

Glossary
_____

boss: a person who is in charge and tells people what work to do

service: the help that people in a store or restaurant give to you

plan: something you decide to do

invest: give money to a bank or company so you get more money later

early: before the usual or expected time

advertise: use photos, videos, or words to try to tell people to buy something

---

C. Listen to the presentation about starting a business. Complete the tips the speaker gives.

1. First, decide on a _____ .

2. Second, do some _____ .

3. Next, make a _____ .

4. After that, check _____ .

5. Next, advertise _____ .

6. Then _____ .

7. After some time, _____ .

8. Then decide _____ .

D. Listen again. Complete the sentences.

1. The presentation is about _____ .

2. The presenter has _____ tips to have a successful business.

3. The first tip is to think of an _____ . Do you want the business to sell a _____ or a _____ ?

4. People do better in business when they _____ what they do.

5. Find out how many other companies have your _____ idea.

6. Start to _____
_____ now.

7. Make a _____ .

8. Check your _____ .

9. Ask yourself some _____ .

10. Decide the next _____ to make your business better.

STEP 2: PREPARE TO SPEAK

A. Read the presentation. Circle all the sequence words and underline all the instructions. The first one is done for you.

So, you want to be your own boss? Well, you are in the right place. This presentation is about starting your own business. Please look at your handout. I will share eight tips with you today. If you follow these instructions, you will have a successful business! (First,) decide on a business idea. What do you want to sell? A service or a product? Think of something you like to do. People do better in business when they like what they do. Second, do some research. Find out how many other companies have your same idea. Learn how they do their business. Next, make a business plan. Think about the kinds of services or products your company will have. After that, check your money. How much do you have to invest in the business? Start early and save money now! Next, advertise your business. Make a website, print some business cards, tell everyone about your company. Then begin! After some time, ask yourself questions. For example: How can I make my business better? Do I need more workers or different products? Then decide your next step to make your business better.

B. Think of a process or activity you want to teach to your classmates. Choose an idea from the box or think of your own.

how to save money or time	how to find a good job
how to find a good university	how to learn more English
how to study for a test	how to make a lot of money
how to be a good student	how to start an online business

C. Write the activity or process. Then write the instructions. Use imperatives and sequence words.

Activity or Process _____

Instructions

STEP 3: SPEAK

A. Practice your presentation.

1. Look up as you give the instructions.

2. Speak clearly.

3. Show pictures or use gestures to explain the instructions.

B. Work in a group of four students. Take turns giving your instructions to the group.

STEP 4: PEER FEEDBACK

Write two of your group members' names in the chart. Listen to the presentations. Complete the chart with the information from each presentation.

Classmates' Names	Activity or Process	Instructions

BUILDING VOCABULARY

UNDERSTANDING AND USING JOB-SEARCH VOCABULARY

These words and phrases are related to finding a job.

A. Look at the pictures and read the descriptions. Write the matching words from the box. Ask your classmates for help with any words you don't know.

application	employee	interview	résumé (curriculum vitae)
cover letter	employer	job search	

1. _____: when a person looks for a job

2. _____: a paper you complete to ask for a job or get into school

3. _____: a list of the schools you went to, the jobs you had

4. _____: a letter or email you send with your résumé when you look for a job

5. _____: to ask someone questions to see if they are good enough for a job or a school

6. _____: a person you work for

7. _____: worker who gets paid for work

B. Read the conversations. Write the missing words.

1. A: My _____ is great. She lets us leave early on Friday afternoons.

   B: I want a boss like that!

2. A: How is the _____ going? Do you have a job yet?

   B: It's going well. But I don't have a job yet.

3. A: I go for my _____ on Monday.

   B: Do you know what type of questions they ask?

(Continued)

4. A: The _____ for that job is long. I had to write five pages!

   B: I hope you get the job!

5. A: Do you work at that company?

   B: Yes, I am an _____ there.

6. A: What do I write in a _____?

   B: You tell company why you want the job.

7. A: What information do I put on my _____?

   B: Write all the schools you went to and all the jobs you had.

C. Discuss the questions with a partner.

1. Do you have a résumé / curriculum vitae? What do information do you have on it?

2. Tell about your employer now (or an employer that you had in the past).

3. Tell about a job application that you completed.

4. Tell about an interview that you had.

5. Where are some places to begin a job search?

⚙ Go to **MyEnglishLab** to complete a vocabulary practice.

APPLY YOUR SKILLS

In this chapter, you listened to a sales presentation about 3-D printers and how they can help business. You listened to a talk about how to start your own business. You gave instructions for an activity or a process. In Apply Your Skills, you will listen to a conversation about successful businesses. You will think of and present instructions for how to be successful at something.

VOCABULARY PREVIEW

A. Read the sentences. Look at the boldfaced words and phrases. Do you know what they mean? Share your ideas with a partner.

1. I finish school **soon**.
2. I am **able to** use a 3-D printer.
3. It is good to **apply** to many jobs.
4. What **college** do you go to?
5. Many people **compete** for the same jobs.
6. Make a **list** of the skills you know how to do.
7. It is important to be **honest** on your résumé.
8. What **type** of skills do you have?
9. I am good at **technology**. I like to work with computers.
10. **Communication** is important in business.

B. Write the boldfaced words and phrases from Part A next to their definitions.

_____ 1. a set of items that you write one below the other

_____ 2. try to win or get something

_____ 3. ask to work at a company or study at a university

_____ 4. a particular kind of person or thing

_____ 5. in a short time from now

_____ 6. a place where people study; university

_____ 7. the knowledge and equipment used in science

_____ 8. not lying, cheating, or stealing

_____ 9. can do something

_____ 10. the act of speaking or writing to someone

⊙ Go to **MyEnglishLab** to complete a vocabulary practice.

PREDICT

Look at the pictures. Think about the speaker, the situation, and the topic. Then predict the words and phrases you will hear. Complete the chart.

Speaker	
Situation	
Topic	
Words and Phrases	

LISTEN

🔊 **A. Listen. Were your predictions correct? Which ones? Tell a partner.**

My prediction was correct / incorrect about …

B. Circle the ideas the presenter talks about.

Everyone is looking for a job at the same time.

Make a list of your skills.

Don't compete with other people.

Soft skills are important.

Practice interview skills.

It's important to have a plan.

Learn new skills.

Learn a language.

C. Listen to the excerpts from the presentation. Complete the tasks.

SECTION 1

1. What is Rachel's job?

   a. She helps students apply to university.

   b. She is a university professor.

   c. She helps university students find jobs.

2. The students are from _____ .

   a. different countries

   b. the United States

   c. the United Arab Emirates

3. When will the students finish school?

   a. They finished last year.

   b. They will finish soon.

   c. They will finish next year.

SECTION 2

4. By the year 2033, computers or robots will do _____ of all jobs.

   a. 4%

   b. 70%

   c. 47%

5. To find a job, Rachel says the first step is to _____ .

   a. make a plan to learn new skills

   b. make a list of your skills

   c. write a letter to the company

SECTION 3

6. The two types of skills Rachel talks about are _____.

   a. study skills and work skills

   b. hard skills and soft skills

   c. business skills and technology skills

7. Being a good leader is an example of a _____.

   a. hard skill

   b. soft skill

8. Employers wants people who have _____.

   a. mostly hard skills

   b. mostly soft skills

   c. both hard and soft skills

LISTEN AGAIN

A. Number the instructions in the order the presenter gives them.

   _____ Write the skills you still need.

   _____ Be honest.

   _____ Write the skills you do well.

   _____ Have a plan.

   _____ Make a list.

   _____ Learn new skills.

   _____ Look at your list.

B. Listen to how the presenter recommends making a list. Make your own list below. Write the skills you have and the skills you need. Remember to write the hard skills and the soft skills (from pages 154–155). Then share your list with a partner.

Skills I have	Skills I need

VOCABULARY REVIEW

Complete the sentences with words from the box.

able	college		compete	list	technology
apply	communication		honest	soon	type

1. _____ is an important skill to do well. It's important to talk to people.

2. It's a good idea to make a _____ of all the skills you have.

3. I go to a small _____ in New York City. I study business.

4. Many people _____ for the same jobs. It's important to tell about your skills.

5. Employers always look to see if you have _____ skills. Computers are a big part of business.

6. There are two _____ of skills: hard skills and soft skills.

7. Many students _____ for a job after they finish school.

8. I finish school _____. I'm excited to get a job.

9. Frederica wasn't _____ on her application. Now the boss thinks she knows how to use the 3-D printer.

10. I'm sorry. I am not _____ to come to the job interview this afternoon.

THINK VISUALLY

Technology is good, but it also changes business. In some areas of business, new technology means fewer jobs for people. Which jobs are most at risk? Look at the chart and answer the questions on the next page.

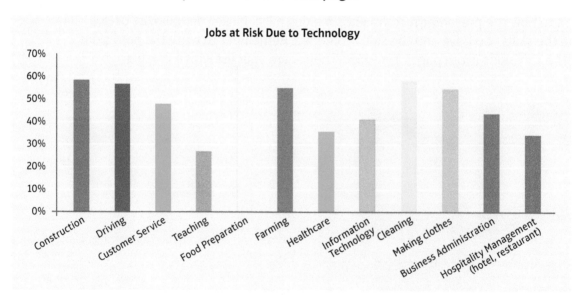

Jobs at Risk Due to Technology

1. Which job is at the most risk? Why do you think that is true?

2. Which job is at the least risk? Why do you think that is true?

3. How does teaching compare to cleaning?

4. How does hospitality management compare to customer service?

5. Which job is the most surprising to you? Why?

GRAMMAR

USING IMPERATIVES

Work with a partner. Look at the chart in Think Visually. Which types of business are you interested in? Are they low risk or high risk? Use imperatives to make recommendations about getting jobs. Use the examples to help you.

A: I want to work in the healthcare business.

B: Yes. Look for a job in the healthcare business. It is low risk. How about you?

A: I'm interested in construction.

B: Don't do construction! It is high risk.

ASSIGNMENT

Give instructions for how to do a skill.

PREPARE TO SPEAK

A. Think of a skill you are good at or choose a skill from the box.

how to play a sport or a game	how to learn English online
how to make a website	how to use a cell phone app
how to communicate with your boss	how to take great photos
how to be a good employee	how to get experience for your career
how to be a good boss	

B. Think about the skill you chose. Write the steps for the instructions in the chart. Use sequence words and imperatives.

Steps	
1.	
2.	
3.	
4.	
5.	
6.	

SPEAK

A. Present your instructions to the class or to a group.

B. Listen to your classmates' presentations. Choose one classmate's skill you want to learn. Then listen and and complete the chart.

Classmate's Name	Skill	Instructions

🔊 Go to **MyEnglishLab** to complete grammar and vocabulary practices.

DEVELOP SOFT SKILLS

USING GRAPHIC ORGANIZERS TO STUDY VOCABULARY

When you learn a new language, you need to remember many new words. Graphic organizers can help you organize new words, so you can review and remember them better. Reviewing new words helps you remember them so you can use them.

Glossary

experience: knowledge or skill that you get from doing a job

remind: cause a person to remember something or to think of someone

review: prepare for a test by studying things again

A. Look at the examples of graphic organizers. Do you use any of them to study new vocabulary? Read the descriptions. Then answer the questions.

Use a **word web** to learn several words about the same topic.

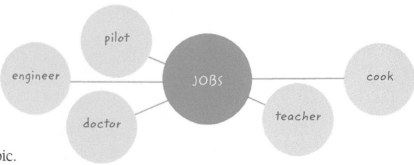

Use a **word map** to list information about a word.

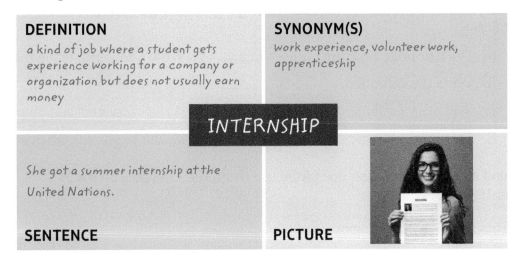

DEFINITION
a kind of job where a student gets experience working for a company or organization but does not usually earn money

SYNONYM(S)
work experience, volunteer work, apprenticeship

INTERNSHIP

SENTENCE
She got a summer internship at the United Nations.

PICTURE

Use a **Venn diagram** to compare two or more words.

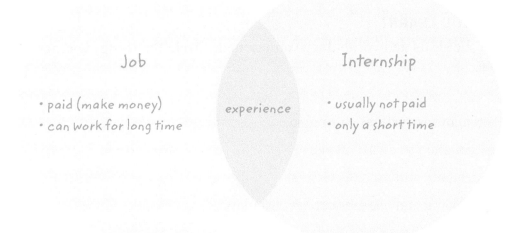

Job

• paid (make money)
• can work for long time

experience

Internship

• usually not paid
• only a short time

1. Which graphic organizer is best to learn a lot of words about the same topic?

   _____

2. Which graphic organizer is best to learn the differences and similarities between two words?

   _____

3. Which graphic organizer is best to learn a lot about each word?

   _____

B. Listen to two university students, Asad and Duong, talking about studying vocabulary. Number the instructions for making a graphic organizer in the correct order.

_____ a. Draw or print a picture. _____ e. Write a sentence using the word.

_____ b. Write the definition. _____ f. Review the information.

_____ c. Write the vocabulary word. _____ g. Write synonyms and antonyms.

_____ d. Decide which words to study. _____ h. Make the graphic organizer.

C. What kind of graphic organizer does Asad use (from the examples on pages 154 and 155)?

_____

D. Practice using a graphic organizer. Choose five new words you want to study from this chapter. Follow the instructions in Part C. Then compare graphic organizers with a partner.

WHAT DID YOU LEARN?

Check (✓) the skills and vocabulary you learned. Circle the things you need to practice.

SKILLS

☐ I can listen for instructions and steps.

☐ I can ask for and give instructions.

☐ I can understand and use imperatives.

☐ I can understand and use job-search vocabulary.

☐ I can use graphic organizers to study vocabulary.

VOCABULARY

☐ able	☐ cut	☐ save time
☐ application	☐ employer / employee	☐ size
☐ apply	☐ honest	☐ soon
☐ begin	☐ interview	☐ steps
☐ college	☐ job search	☐ technology
☐ communication	☐ like	☐ type
☐ compete	☐ list	☐ work
☐ correct	☐ objects	☐ résumé / curriculum vitae
☐ cover letter	☐ save money	

◐ Go to **MyEnglishLab** to complete a self-assessment.

◐ Go to **MyEnglishLab** for a challenge listening about Business and Technology.

Psychology

Go to **MyEnglishLab** to see an introduction about **PSYCHOLOGY**.

| Chapter 7 | **On Time** |

CHAPTER PROFILE

Psychology is the study of the mind and how it works. Psychologists study how people think and behave.

You will listen to

• a podcast about different ideas of time.

• conversations about finding a roommate.

• a discussion about time in different cultures.

You will also

• role-play a conversation about finding a roommate.

• have a group discussion about your opinions of time.

OUTCOMES

• Listen for reasons

• Ask follow-up questions

• Use *because* and *because of* with reasons

• Tell time

• Understand cultural attitudes about personal space

For more about **PSYCHOLOGY**, see Chapter 8. See also ⟦RW⟧ **PSYCHOLOGY**, Chapters 7 and 8.

GETTING STARTED

A. Read the information. Answer the questions. Then compare with a partner.

1. You're meeting a friend at a restaurant at 6:30 P.M.

   What time do you arrive? _____

2. Your bus to the university leaves at 7:05 A.M.

   What time do you arrive at the bus stop? _____

3. Your class starts at 8:00 A.M.

   What time do you arrive in the classroom? _____

4. Your job starts at 3:00 P.M.

   What time do you arrive at work? _____

5. You have a project due next Friday.

   What day do you give it to your teacher? _____

6. You're going to see a movie that starts at 7:00 P.M.

   What time do you get to the theater? _____

B. Read these excuses (reasons) for being late. Do you ever use these excuses? Check (✓) the ones you used in the past. Write two more ideas. Then compare with a partner.

☐ The bus / train was late.   ☐ There was a lot of traffic (cars on the road).

☐ The weather / driving was bad.   ☐ My computer broke.

☐ My car broke down.   ☐ I stopped to help a friend / neighbor.

☐ My alarm clock did not work.

My idea: _____

My idea: _____

C. How important is it to be on time? Circle your opinion. Then tell the class. Do most students agree?

Not important at all   A little important   Important   Very important

⊙ **Go to MyEnglishLab to complete a self-assessment.**

LISTEN

SKILL: LISTENING FOR REASONS

People give reasons to explain their ideas. We use special words and phrases to introduce reasons. Listening for these words and phrases will help you understand reasons and explanations.

Words / Phrases for Introducing Reasons	Examples
because	She was late for class **because** her bicycle broke.
That's because …	Tom wakes up early every day. **That's because** he walks to work.
That is why …	There were a lot of cars on the road. **That is why** I was late.
One reason is …	I don't wear a watch. **One reason is** I use the clock on my cell phone.
The reason is …	There are no trains today. **The reason is** the weather.

PRONUNCIATION NOTE

🔊 **Listen and repeat the sentences.**

Speakers often shorten the word *because* to *'cause* (pronounced /kəz/). Listen and read along with these sentences.

1. She wasn't in class because she was sick.
2. They got an A on the project because they worked very hard.
3. I'm late for class because I was talking to my friends.

🔊 **Listen to the conversations. Complete the tasks.**

1. Circle the gist of Conversation 1.

   a. not doing homework

   b. being late for class

   c. having a busy schedule

2. What words and phrases do you hear for giving reasons? Circle all the ones you hear.

   because   That's because …   That is why …

   The reason is …   One reason is …

3. What reasons does the speaker give for being late?

   Monday: _____

   Yesterday: _____

   Today: _____

4. Circle the gist of Conversation 2.

   a. playing video games with roommates

   b. what makes a good roommate

   c. why the speaker does not like his roommate

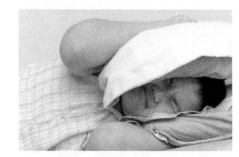

5. What words and phrases do you hear for giving reasons? Circle all you hear.

because   That's because …   That is why …

The reason is …   One reason is …

6. Read the questions. Write the reasons.

Why doesn't the speaker like his new roommate? _____

Why is he always tired? _____

REMEMBER

Complete the sentence.

People give reasons to _____ their ideas.

Write three sentences to explain why you study English. Use three different words or phrases for introducing reasons.

_____ .

_____ .

_____ .

VOCABULARY PREVIEW

A. Read the sentences. Look at the boldfaced words and phrases. Do you know what they mean? Share your ideas with a partner.

1. I need to **organize** my desk. There are papers everywhere.

2. Don't be late for class. The teacher always starts **on time**.

3. A: When will you arrive at the meeting?

    B: **It depends** when the bus arrives.

4. Do you **prefer** to sleep late or wake up early on weekends?

5. My sister and I have a good **relationship**. She is my best friend.

6. My parents are **angry** when I am late for dinner.

7. What is the **schedule** for Saturday? What time do we start and finish?

8. I can only do one thing **at a time**. I feel stressed when I do too much.

9. I feel more **comfortable** when I arrive early.

10. A: **Several** people were late for class today.

    B: Yes, Malik, Avery, Roberto, and Susana were late.

B. Write the boldfaced words from Part A next to their definitions.

_____ 1. during one moment

_____ 2. a plan of what you will do and when you will do it

_____ 3. a phrase that means you are not sure about something

_____ 4. relaxed; not worried

_____ 5. arrange in order neatly

_____ 6. like something more than something else

_____ 7. more than two but not many

_____ 8. not late; arrives or happens when it should

_____ 9. a connection between people, for example, friends

_____ 10. feeling very upset; annoyed

C. You will hear these sentences and phrases in the listening. Read them aloud with a partner. Do you remember the meanings of the boldfaced words?

1. We use time every day. It helps us **organize** our lives.

2. Are you always **on time** to meetings?

3. How do you feel when you are late? **It depends** on your idea of time.

4. Some people **prefer** to arrive early. Other people like to arrive right on time.

5. These different ideas about time can make problems in our **relationships**.

6. My mother often got **angry**.

7. People who think **schedules** are important, like my mother, like to start and end on time.

8. For this reason, these people prefer to do one thing **at a time**.

9. This is because being on time makes them feel **comfortable**.

10. These people often think about and do **several** things at one time.

↻ Go to **MyEnglishLab** to complete a vocabulary practice.

PREDICT

Look at the pictures. Think about the speakers, the situation, and the topic. Then predict the words or phrases you will hear. Complete the chart on the next page.

LATE OR EARLY?

How We Think about Time

Speakers	
Situation	
Topic	
Words and Phrases	

Glossary

stick to: continue doing something.

excuse: a reason you give when you do something wrong

LISTEN

🔊 A. Listen. Check (✓) if your predictions are correct or incorrect. For any that are incorrect, write the correct information.

	Correct	Incorrect	Correct Information
Speakers			
Situation			
Topic			
Words and Phrases			

B. Circle the gist of the podcast.

a. how to work well with other people

b. how to be on time for meetings

c. reasons why people are late

d. different ways of thinking about time

🔊 C. Listen to the excerpts from the podcast. Complete the tasks.

SECTION 1

1. What is the speaker's job?

    a. She helps people with relationships.

    b. She teaches at a university.

    c. She is a doctor at a hospital.

2. Why does she say that time is important?

    a. It helps us organize our lives.

    b. People have different ideas about it.

    c. Most people prefer to be on time.

3. People's ideas about time can make problems with _____.

    a. meetings

    b. health

    c. relationships

SECTION 2

4. The speaker's mother said, _____

    a. "On time is good. Late is bad."

    b. "Late is on time. On time is good."

    c. "Early is on time. On time is late."

5. The speaker's parents _____ .

    a. feel the same way about time

    b. disagree about time

    c. don't think schedules are important

6. To solve the problem, her parents _____ .

    a. never go out

    b. take a taxi

    c. drive two cars

SECTION 3

7. Why do some people prefer to do one thing at a time?

    a. because they get tired easily

    b. because they do things slowly

    c. because they like to start and end on time

8. Being on time makes these people feel _____ .

    a. stressed

    b. comfortable

    c. angry

9. The speaker says people who are often late _____ .

    a. usually have a reason or an excuse

    b. never finish anything

    c. are more helpful to their friends

LISTEN AGAIN

Listen again. Read the sentences. Circle *T* (true) or *F* (false). Correct the false statements.

T / F   1. Helga Shumaker wrote a book called *Early Is on Time. On Time Is Late.*

_____

T / F   2. How often people are late depends on their idea of time.

_____

T / F   3. Most people have the same idea about time.

_____

T / F   4. Shumaker thinks time is sometimes a reason for relationship problems.

_____

T / F   5. People who feel it is OK to be late often make lists of things to do.

_____

VOCABULARY REVIEW

Complete the sentences with words and phrases from the box.

angry	comfortable	on time	prefer	schedule
at a time	it depends	organize	relationship	several

1. There are _____ people in my class who always come late.

2. A: Do you want to take the bus to the theater?

   B: I _____ to take a taxi. It's faster.

3. When you are busy, can you do more than one thing _____?

4. I have a very busy _____ today. I have three classes. Then I have to work.

5. I don't know what time we will arrive. _____ on the weather and the traffic.

6. Does Geraldo have a good _____ with his brother?

7. Let's leave now. I want to get to the meeting _____ .

8. I have to work late. I need to _____ these photos for my presentation.

9. Carla wants a roommate. She does not feel _____ living alone.

10. My boss doesn't get _____ when people come late.

● Go to **MyEnglishLab** for more listening practice.

SPEAK

SKILL: ASKING FOLLOW-UP QUESTIONS

A conversation usually involves questions and answers. When someone gives us information or tells a story, we can ask follow-up questions to get more information and to continue the conversation. Use the examples to help you.

Follow-up Questions

What happened?	What do you think?	Where … ?
How was it?	What about … ?	When … ?
What did you do then?	Who … ?	Why … ?
Tell me more about …	What … ?	How … ?

> **TIP**
>
> When someone is speaking, it is important to show that you are listening. This lets the speaker know that you are interested in the conversation. Here are some phrases you can use to show that you are listening.
>
> | | | | |
> |---|---|---|---|
> | I see. | Really? | Yes. | I understand. |
> | Of course. | Oh. | Uh-huh. / Mm hm. | Wow. |

A. Read the conversation. Underline the follow-up questions. Circle the phrases that show that the listener is listening. Then practice the conversation with a partner.

A: Oh, no! I can't be late for class! Professor Smith will be angry.

B: Why?

A: Because I was late two times last week.

B: Oh. What happened?

A: Well, on Monday I was late because my alarm clock didn't work.

B: I see. When was the next time?

A: Wednesday. I was late again because of the traffic.

B: Wow. Well, you better get to class on time today!

B. Choose one of these questions and ask your partner. Ask three follow-up questions to continue the conversation. Remember to use phrases to show that you are listening.

What do you do in your free time?	What is your school / work schedule?
Were you late for something this week?	What makes you angry?
Do you prefer to be on time? Why?	
Do you have a busy schedule this week?	
Do you have any meetings this week?	

REMEMBER

Write two reasons why it's important ask follow-up questions.

_____.

_____.

What are three follow-up questions you can use in a conversation?

_____?

_____?

_____?

What are three phrases you can use to show that you are listening?

_____   _____   _____

Grammar for Speaking | Using *because* and *because of* with reasons

We use *because* and *because of* to introduce reasons.

RULES	EXAMPLES
We use a verb phrase (subject and verb) after *because*.	She was confused **because** the meeting started late.
We use a noun after *because of*.	The bus was late **because of** the rain.

GRAMMAR NOTE

Both *because* and *because of* can come at the beginning of the sentence or in the middle of the sentence. If used at the beginning of the sentence, use a comma after the first clause.

I always wake up early **because** I have noisy roommates.
Because I have noisy roommates, I always wake up early.
Giles missed several classes **because of** his sickness.
Because of his sickness, Giles missed several classes.

When speaking, you can use these clauses alone.
A: Why didn't you come to class?
B: <u>Because</u> I was sick.

However, in formal writing, we do not use simple clauses with *because* or *because of*.
~~Because I was sick.~~

A. Complete the sentences with *because* or *because of*.

1. I was late for class _____ the traffic on the roads.

2. Marta can't go to work today _____ she has a doctor appointment.

3. The teacher was angry _____ several students were late.

4. The plane arrived late _____ the storm.

5. _____ it was rainy, I drove my car to work.

6. _____ my new work schedule, I can meet you for lunch anytime.

B. Write sentences with *because or because of*. Then take turns reading your sentences aloud with a partner.

1. the weather / I want to leave early.

   _____.

2. Thomas gets up early. / He goes to the gym before class.

   _____.

3. The teacher was angry. / Everyone was late.

   _____.

4. I don't know what time I will arrive / my busy schedule

   _____.

5. vacation / There are no students on campus.

   _____.

6. Keiko's report was late. / Her computer broke.

   _____.

7. I will be late for dinner / the meeting

   _____.

8. the new university rules / The teacher can't change the class time.

   _____.

C. Read the conversation starters. Write an answer with *because* or *because of*. Then practice the conversations with a partner. Use phrases to show you are listening and ask follow-up questions to keep the conversation going.

1. A: Why do you prefer to be early?

   B: _____

2. A: Why were you late for work yesterday?

   B: _____

3. A: Why do you wake up early?

   B: _____

4. A: Why are you so tired?

   B: _____

5. A: Why can't you come to dinner tonight?

   B: _____

⊙ Go to **MyEnglishLab** for more grammar practice.

ROLE-PLAY: FINDING A ROOMMATE

STEP 1: LISTEN BEFORE YOU SPEAK

A. Look at the pictures. Think about the speakers, the situation, and the topic. Then predict the words and phrases you will hear. Complete the chart.

Speakers	
Situation	
Topic	
Words and Phrases	

B. Read the words and definitions. You will hear these words in the listening.

Glossary

grades: scores the teacher gives on a test or on your school work
active: doing many things
fun: happy, enjoyable

C. Listen to the conversation. Complete the tasks and answer the questions.

1. Circle the gist of the conversation.

a. A student is changing his class schedule.

b. A student wants to play basketball.

c. A student is looking for a roommate.

2. What type of roommate is Jamal looking for?

_____

3. What time does Jamal wake up?

   a. very early

   b. very late

   c. around 9:00

4. What does Jamal do in the morning?

   a. He studies.

   b. He exercises.

   c. He goes to class.

5. Why does Jamal study a lot?

   a. because he does not have any hobbies

   b. because he does not get good grades

   c. because he wants to join the basketball team

6. Who is Kevin Parker?

   a. Jamal's new roommate

   b. a member of the basketball team

   c. a student in one of Jamal's classes

🔊 **D. Listen to the conversation. Answer the questions.**

1. What type of roommate is Irena looking for?

   _____

   _____

2. What does Irena do in her free time?

   a. She studies.

   b. She is in several clubs.

   c. She visits her friends' rooms.

3. When does she study?

   a. after class

   b. during dinner

   c. late at night

STEP 2: PREPARE TO SPEAK

A. You are going to role-play finding a roommate. Read the audio scripts from Step 1. Follow these instructions:

1. Underline the sentences that give reasons.

2. Circle the follow-up questions.

CONVERSATION 1

Jamal:	Good morning. I'm Jamal.
Advisor:	Hi, Jamal. So, what kind of roommate are you looking for?
Jamal:	Well, I study a lot. That is why I want a quiet roommate.
Advisor:	OK. Tell me about your schedule.
Jamal:	Well, I go to bed early because I have a busy schedule.
Advisor:	I see. What time do you wake up?
Jamal:	Around 5:00 A.M.
Advisor:	Wow. That's very early.
Jamal:	Yes. The reason is I go to the gym every morning.
Advisor:	Oh. Do you play sports?
Jamal:	Yes. I want to join the basketball team. Because I need good grades to be on the team, I have to study a lot.
Advisor:	Uh huh.
Jamal:	That's why I want a quiet roommate.
Advisor:	I understand. Well, I know a student who needs a roommate. His name is Kevin Parker.
Jamal:	Kevin Parker? Really? The best player on the basketball team?
Advisor:	Yes.
Jamal:	Wow …

CONVERSATION 2

Advisor: Hello. What's your name?

Irena: I'm Irena.

Advisor: What kind of roommate do you want, Irena?

Irena: Well, because I'm very active, I want a fun roommate.

Advisor: I'm sorry. Can you repeat that?

Irena: Yes. I want a fun roommate because I don't like to be bored.

Advisor: I see. What do you do in your free time?

Irena: I have a lot of interests. That's why I am in several clubs.

Advisor: Uh huh. Which clubs?

Irena: I'm in the hiking club, the volleyball club, and the business club.

Advisor: Wow! When do you study?

Irena: My friends come to my room after dinner. We stay up late and study together.

Advisor: OK. We'll do our best to find you the perfect roommate.

B. Practice Conversation 1 with a partner. Then change partners and practice Conversation 2.

C. Write answers to the questions. Use *because* or *because of* for reasons.

1. Do you have a busy schedule? Why or why not?

_____

2. Do you like to wake up early? Why or why not?

_____

3. Do you like to stay up late? Why or why not?

_____

4. What do you do in your free time?

_____

5. When and where do you prefer to study?

_____

6. What kind of roommate is good for you? Why?

_____

STEP 3: SPEAK

Interview three classmates. Ask the questions from Step 2, Part C and complete the chart. Remember to ask follow-up questions.

	Classmate 1		Classmate 2		Classmate 3	
	Name:		Name:		Name:	
Schedule	☐ Busy	☐ Not busy	☐ Busy	☐ Not busy	☐ Busy	☐ Not busy
	Reason:		Reason:		Reason:	
Wake up early?	☐ Yes	☐ No	☐ Yes	☐ No	☐ Yes	☐ No
	Reason:		Reason:		Reason:	
Stay up late?	☐ Yes	☐ No	☐ Yes	☐ No	☐ Yes	☐ No
	Reason:		Reason:		Reason:	
Free time						
Prefers to study	When: Where:		When: Where:		When: Where:	
Type of roommate						

BUILDING VOCABULARY

TELLING TIME

Telling time is an important skill. There are different ways to express the time in English. It is useful to know and practice these phrases so you can understand and give the time correctly.

When the clock is on the hour, we say "o'clock.":

It's one **o'clock**.

There are different ways to say this time:

1. It's four ten.

2. It's ten **after** four.

3. It's ten **past** four.

There are different ways to say this time:

1. It's two-fifty.

2. It's ten **to** three.

3. It's ten **before** three.

When the time is 15 minutes before or after the hour, we can also say "quarter."
That is because 15 minutes is one quarter (1/4) of an hour.

1. It's ten-fifteen.

2. It's quarter **past** ten.

3. It's quarter **after** ten.

(Continued)

1. It's ten-forty-five.

2. It's quarter **to** eleven.

When the time is 30 minutes after the hour, we can also say "half past."
That is because 30 minutes is one half (1/2) of an hour.

1. It's six-thirty.

2. It's half **past** six.

A. Work with a partner. Complete the chart with different ways to say the times.

	Times	How to Say the Time	
1.	7:10	seven-ten	
2.	5:40		twenty to six
3.	1:25	one-twenty-five	
4.	5:55		five before six
5.	11:30	eleven-thirty	
6.	2:45	two-forty-five	
7.	9:50		ten to ten
8.	4:00		–

B. Listen and check your answers. Then practice saying the times with a partner.

CULTURE NOTE

Speakers of British English usually don't use the phrase "half past." They often say: "Half _____." For example, "It's half eight." means "It's 8:30."

Many cultures use the 24-hour clock for schedules. For example:

1:00 P.M. = 13:00   2:30 P.M. = 14:30   3:45 P.M. = 15:45

VOCABULARY NOTE

When we express time under 10 minutes past the hour, we usually say the letter "O" in front of the number:

6:08 = "six o eight"   10:01 = "ten o one"

Many times, people don't say the exact time. They give the closest time.

For example:

A: What time is it?   A: What time is it?

B: It's almost 4:30.   B: It's about 4:30. OR It's around 4:30.

Special time expressions:

12:00 A.M. = midnight   12:00 P.M. = noon

C. **Listen to the conversations. Write the times you hear. Use numbers. For example, 5:15.**

1. _____   6. _____

2. _____   7. _____

3. _____   8. _____

4. _____   9. _____

5. _____   10. _____

D. **Listen again. Write the questions for asking the time.**

1. A: _____   6. A: _____

   B: It's five after two.   B: Twenty past twelve.

2. A: _____   7. A: _____

   B: Yes, it's quarter to nine.   B: Yes, it's twenty to seven.

3. A: _____   8. A: _____

   B: Sure, it's ten to five.   B: Noon.

4. A: _____   9. A: _____

   B: It's half past six.   B: I do. It's quarter past eight.

5. A: _____   10. A: _____

   B: Twenty-five to three.   B: Let me see. It's five to six.

E. **Work with a partner. Choose Chart A or B. Don't look at your partner's chart. Take turns asking for the times. Write the times your partner says. Then compare charts. Are the times correct? Use the example to help you.**

   A: Excuse me. What time is it?

   B: It's half past two.

   A: Thank you.

CHART A

	Tell your partner these times.	Write your partner's times.
1.	3:25	
2.	4:45	
3.	11:20	
4.	6:50	
5.	8:05	
6.	1:35	
7.	8:30	
8.	5:15	

(Continued)

CHART B

	Tell your partner these times.	Write your partner's times.
1.	5:10	
2.	2:40	
3.	12:15	
4.	9:30	
5.	3:55	
6.	10:45	
7.	1:25	
8.	4:35	

F. **Work with a partner. Ask and answer the questions.**

1. What time does this class begin?

2. What time does it finish?

3. What time is it now?

4. What time do you eat lunch?

5. What time did you get home yesterday?

6. What time did you arrive in class today?

⬆ Go to **MyEnglishLab** to complete a vocabulary practice.

APPLY YOUR SKILLS

In this chapter, you listened to a podcast about different ideas of time. You did a role play about finding a good roommate. In Apply Your Skills, you will listen to a discussion about how different cultures think about time. Then you will have a group discussion about your opinions of time.

VOCABULARY PREVIEW

A. Read the sentences. Look at the boldfaced words and phrases. Do you know what they mean? Share your ideas with a partner.

1. In my **culture**, people prefer to be on time.

2. **Most** people are on time for work. Some people are late.

3. My teachers always **follow** the class schedule.

4. I am sometimes late and sometimes early. It depends on the **situation**.

5. Classes **end** at 3:00.

6. I don't like to be late. People **rely on** me.

7. I am always on time for work. In my **personal** life, I am always late.

B. Write the boldfaced words from Part A next to their definitions.

_____ 1. agree with or go along with

_____ 2. finish

_____ 3. trust; believe that someone will do something

_____ 4. the actions happening in a particular place and time

_____ 5. belonging or relating to you and your life

_____ 6. the beliefs, customs, and way of life of a particular people

_____ 7. many; the largest amount

◐ Go to **MyEnglishLab** to complete a vocabulary practice.

PREDICT

Look at the pictures. Think about the speaker, the situation, and the topic. Then predict the words and phrases you will hear. Complete the chart.

Time in Different Cultures

Speaker	
Situation	
Topic	
Words and Phrases	

LISTEN

A. Listen. Were your predictions correct? Which ones? Tell a partner.

My prediction was correct / incorrect about …

B. Complete the tasks.

1. Circle the gist of the discussion.

   a. business around the world

   b. ideas about time in different cultures

   c. what people do with their personal time

2. Which countries are the students from? Check (✔) all the ones you hear.

   ☐ a. Saudi Arabia   ☐ e. The United States

   ☐ b. The United Arab Emirates   ☐ f. Kenya

   ☐ c. Honduras   ☐ g. South Korea

   ☐ d. Canada   ☐ h. Japan

C. Listen to the excerpts from the discussion. Complete the tasks.

SECTION 1

1. What is important in the United Arab Emirates?

   a. relationships

   b. business

   c. meetings

2. In Hassan's country, the schedule says the meeting ends at 2:00. What time will it end?

    a. Right on time.

    b. Long after 2:00.

    c. It depends on the situation.

SECTION 2

3. In Honduras, how do people think about time?

    a. They prefer to start and end things on time.

    b. They finish one thing before they begin something new.

    c. They don't use schedules in their personal lives.

4. The expression "Even time takes time" comes from _____ .

    a. Honduras

    b. Kenya

    c. Japan

5. "Even time takes time" means _____ .

    a. we need enough time to finish something

    b. time is more important than relationships

    c. the time on the clock is very important

SECTION 3

6. Why are schedules important in Japan?

    a. because people do not like to wait

    b. because people rely on you

    c. because relationships are not important

7. Aki says that following schedules _____ .

    a. is difficult for Japanese people

    c. helps businesses have success

    d. makes good relationships

LISTEN AGAIN

🔊 **A. Listen again. Take notes about people's ideas about time in each culture. Then compare with a partner.**

	United Arab Emirates	Honduras	Kenya	Japan
Ideas about time				
Reasons				

B. Work in a group. Discuss the questions.

1. What are most people's ideas about time in your culture? Do you agree with that idea?

2. Which statement do you agree most with?

   Even time takes its time.

   Following schedules makes good relationships.

3. Does your culture have any expressions about time? What are they?

VOCABULARY REVIEW

Complete the sentences with words from the box.

culture	end	follow	most	personal	rely on	situation

1. The class begins at 9:00 A.M. What time does it _____?

2. I can't be late. People _____ me to be on time.

3. Are you often late for _____ meetings? For example: lunch with a friend.

4. I don't like to _____ a schedule. That's why I'm always late.

5. In what _____ is it OK to be late?

6. Some people arrive late to work, but _____ arrive on time.

7. In my _____, we sometimes say, "Time is money."

THINK VISUALLY

There are different time zones in the world. On a map, the starting point for time zones is Greenwich, England. This is called Greenwich Mean Time (GMT).

For cities around the world, we write time zones with the number of hours difference from GMT and "+" (later) or "−" (earlier).

For example,
+ 2 = GMT + 2 hours, or two hours later than GMT.
− 5 = GMT − 5 hours, or five hours earlier than GMT.

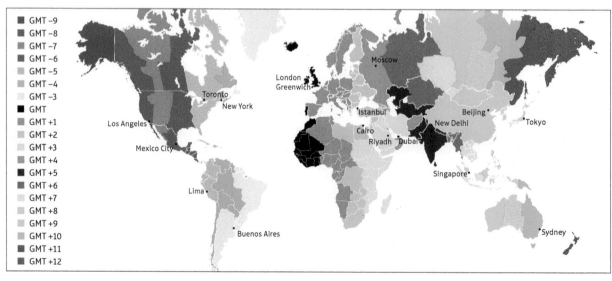

A. Use the time zone map on the previous page to answer the questions.

1. It is 2:00 P.M. in Greenwich. What time is it in New York City? _____

2. It is 6:00 A.M. in Greenwich. What time is it in Dubai? _____

3. It is noon in Greenwich. What time is it in New Delhi? _____

4. It is 11:00 P.M. in Greenwich. What time is it in Los Angeles? _____

5. It is 9:00 A.M. in Beijing. What time is it in Istanbul? _____

6. It is 8:00 P.M. in Mexico City. What time is it in Moscow? _____

7. It is 1:30 P.M. in Cairo. What time is it in Lima? _____

8. It is half past ten in the morning in Tokyo. What time is it in Sydney? _____

9. It is half past noon in Singapore. What time is it in Buenos Aires? _____

10. It is midnight in Toronto. What time is it in Riyadh? _____

B. Ask your partner two questions about the time zones. Use the questions above as an example.

1. It is _____ in _____. What time is it in _____?

2. It is _____ in _____. What time is it in _____?

GRAMMAR

USING *BECAUSE* AND *BECAUSE OF* WITH REASONS

Read the conversations. Rewrite the last line. Use *because or because of.*
Then practice the conversations with a partner.

1. A: We were late to the meeting.

   B: Why?

   A: We wanted to finish our work.

   _____.

2. A: It's difficult to do business in that country.

   B: Why?

   A: Their ideas about time.

   _____.

3. A: Please don't call me after 10:00 P.M.

   B: Why?

   A: The different time zone. It will be 2:00 A.M. in my country.

   _____.

4. A: Our meeting is at 5:30 tomorrow morning.

   B: Why is it so early?

   A: It is 8:30 A.M. in Tehran at that time.

   _____.

5. A: She doesn't like to be late.

   B: Why?

   A: Her culture.

ASSIGNMENT

Have a group discussion. Talk about your opinions and ideas about time and schedules.

PREPARE TO SPEAK

A. Read the situations. Take notes on your opinions and reasons in the chart.

	Situations	Your Opinion	Reasons
1.	Your friend is always 15 minutes late to meet you for dinner. How do you feel about this?		
2.	Today is your first day of work / school. Your bus / train is late. What do you do? How do you feel?		
3.	Your classmate is always late for your study meetings. How do you feel about this?		
4.	You are working with a partner on a big project. He / She thinks about time differently from you. What do you do?		

B. Work with a partner. Talk about your opinions and reasons. Use the examples to help you.

I think … because / because of

In my opinion …

I believe …

I feel …

SPEAK

A. Work with a group of five classmates. Discuss the situations from Prepare to Speak, Part A. Remember to ask follow-up questions and show that you are listening.

B. Listen and take notes on your group member's opinions in the chart on the next page.

Classmates' Names	Situation	Agree / Disagree	Comments

⊙ Go to **MyEnglishLab** to complete grammar and vocabulary practices.

DEVELOP SOFT SKILLS

UNDERSTANDING CULTURAL ATTITUDES ABOUT PERSONAL SPACE

Every country has a unique culture. Culture is the history, beliefs, and traditions of a place, and the attitudes and behaviors of the people who grow up there. Understanding different cultural attitudes is an important part of communication and relationships.

Glossary

imagine: form pictures and ideas in your mind

touching: putting your hand on something or someone

hug: put your arms around someone and hold him or her to show love or friendship

whisper: speak very quietly into someone's ear

aware: If you are aware of something, you know it is happening.

A. Look at the pictures. Who are the people? What is their relationship? Write your ideas. Then compare with a partner.

🎧 **B. Listen to the podcast. Complete the statements with information from the box.**

another culture	international students	research project
friend or family member	personal space	touch or hug

1. The topic of the podcast is _____.

2. The guests of the show are _____.

3. Ali and Santiago worked together on a _____.

4. When you speak to a _____, your circle of personal space can be quite small.

5. Some cultures prefer more personal space. They do not _____ each other as often.

6. It's helpful to understand attitudes about personal space when we meet someone from _____.

🎧 **C. Listen to the next part of the podcast. Read the statements. Circle *T* (true) or *F* (false). Correct the false statements.**

T / F   1. Everyone likes the same amount of personal space.

_____

T / F   2. The amount of personal space depends on your culture.

_____

T / F   3. People in Argentina don't like to be close to each other.

_____

T / F   4. Close friends in Norway stand very close to each other.

_____

T / F   5. Close friends in Saudi Arabia stand at about the same distance as strangers in Norway.

_____

🎧 **D. Listen again. Complete the chart with the information about personal space in different cultures.**

Country	Friends and family	Other people
Saudi Arabia	_____ centimeters / 35.5 inches	_____ meter / 3 feet
Argentina	_____ centimeters / 24 inches	_____ centimeters / 24 inches
Norway	_____ centimeters / 12 inches	_____ meter / 3 feet

E. Read the behaviors. Check (✓) who you are comfortable doing each with. Then compare your answers in a group. Use the example below to help you.

Behavior	Family	Friend	Boss / Professor	Coworker	Stranger
holding hands					
walking arm in arm					
standing or sitting close					
touching (for example, on the arm or shoulder, while talking)					
whispering					

A: In my culture, we are not comfortable holding hands.

B: We sometimes hold hands with family members.

WHAT DID YOU LEARN?

Check (✓) the skills and vocabulary you learned. Circle the things you need to practice.

SKILLS

☐ I can listen for reasons.

☐ I can ask follow-up questions.

☐ I can use *because* and *because of* with reasons.

☐ I can tell time.

☐ I can understand cultural attitudes about personal space.

VOCABULARY

☐ angry	☐ exercise	☐ midnight	☐ relationship
☐ at a time	☐ fixed	☐ most	☐ rely on
☐ club	☐ flexible	☐ noon	☐ schedule
☐ comfortable	☐ follow	☐ on time	☐ several
☐ culture	☐ half past	☐ organize	☐ situation
☐ end	☐ it depends	☐ personal	
☐ excited	☐ meeting	☐ prefer	

⊙ Go to **MyEnglishLab** to complete a self-assessment.

The Habit Cycle

CHAPTER PROFILE

Psychology is the study of how people think and behave. Psychologists study our habits—the behaviors we do often. There are good and bad habits. When you know the habit cycle—how a habit starts—it can help you be more successful.

You will listen to

- a podcast about how habits start and how we can break bad habits.

- a conversation about helping a friend do better in school.

- a talk about habits of successful people.

You will also

- give suggestions to classmates for changing their habits.

- give a presentation about how you spend your time, and make suggestions for managing your time better.

OUTCOMES

- Ask for clarification and repetition
- Make and respond to suggestions
- Use *should / shouldn't* for suggestions
- Recognize and use *-ed* adjectives
- Study for exams

For more about **PSYCHOLOGY**, see Chapter 7. See also [RW] **PSYCHOLOGY**, Chapters 7 and 8.

GETTING STARTED

Habits are activities we do often, sometimes without thinking. Look at the pictures of habits people often have. Write *good habit* or *bad habit* under each picture. Then share your ideas with a partner. Do you have any of the habits?

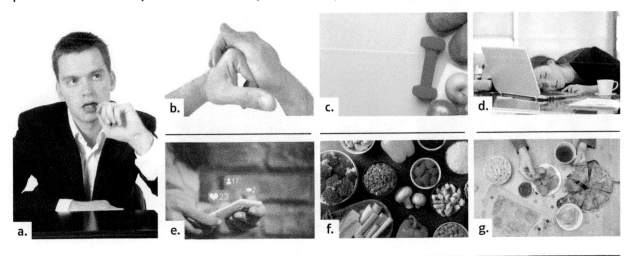

a. b. c. d. e. f. g.

↻ Go to **MyEnglishLab** to complete a self-assessment.

LISTEN

SKILL: ASKING FOR REPETITION AND CLARIFICATION

Speakers often speak quickly. Sometimes they use words or expressions that you do not understand. You may need to stop a speaker to ask them to repeat (say again) or clarify information (explain in a different way). This is called active listening. It is an important skill for understanding. Here are some phrases you can use to be an active listener.

Asking for Repetition	Example
Can you repeat that?	A: I waste a lot of time on social media.
Can you say that again?	B: **What was that?**
What was that?	A: I spend too much time on social media.
Did you say … ?	

Asking for Clarification	Example
What does … mean?	A: Do you have any bad habits?
What do you mean?	B: **What does *habit* mean?**
What do you mean by … ?	A: Habits are activities we do often, sometimes
Do you mean … ?	without thinking.
Are you saying … ?	

🎧 Listen to the conversations. Complete the charts.

CONVERSATION 1

Does the listener ask for repetition or clarification?	
What active listening question does she ask?	
What is the speaker's answer?	

CONVERSATION 2

Does the listener ask for repetition or clarification?	
What active listening question does she ask?	
What is the speaker's answer?	

CONVERSATION 3

Does the listener ask for repetition or clarification?	
What active listening question does he ask?	
What is the speaker's answer?	

REMEMBER

Complete the sentences.

Speakers often speak _____ . Sometimes they use words or expressions that you do not _____ . You may need to stop speakers to ask them _____ (say again) or _____ information (explain in a different way). This is called _____ .

Write three ways to ask for repetition.

_____

_____

_____

Write three ways to ask for clarification.

_____

_____

_____

VOCABULARY PREVIEW

A. Read the sentences. Look at the boldfaced words. Do you know what they mean? Share your ideas with a partner.

1. I eat too much chocolate. Do you have a bad **habit**?

2. Parisa is **stressed** about her job. She has a lot of problems with her boss.

3. My friends eat **unhealthy** foods like hamburgers, fried chicken, and cookies.

4. I **spend** too much money. Every week I spend $40 on coffee.

5. She doesn't study **enough**. She needs to study more.

6. There is nothing to do. I am so **bored**.

7. Be careful. Eating a lot of sweets can **become** a habit.

8. It is **possible** to eat healthy at school. Just bring healthy snacks to class.

9. Can you **fix** the problem with my computer?

10. **Instead** of a hamburger, I want chicken, please.

B. Write the boldfaced words from Part A next to their definitions.

_____ 1. something that you always do, without thinking about it

_____ 2. repair something, make something better

_____ 3. feeling of worry because of problems in your life

_____ 4. not good for your body

_____ 5. begin to be something

_____ 6. in place of someone or something else

_____ 7. able to be done, happen or exist

_____ 8. not interested in anything

_____ 9. use money to buy things

_____ 10. what you need

C. You will hear these sentences in the listening. Read them aloud with a partner. Do you remember the meanings of the boldfaced words?

1. Today we are talking about **habits**.

2. When I feel **stressed**, I eat too much.

3. What are some examples of **unhealthy** habits?

4. They **spend** too much money or don't sleep **enough**.

5. For example, feeling stressed, worried, **bored**, angry, or tired.

6. It **becomes** a bad habit when they do it too much.

7. Is it **possible** to break a bad habit?

8. First, you need to **fix** the problem.

9. **Instead** of bad habits, find healthy things to do.

⊙ Go to **MyEnglishLab** to complete a vocabulary practice.

PREDICT

Look at the pictures. Think about the speaker, the situation, and the topic. Then predict the words and phrases you will hear. Compare your ideas with a partner.

AUPod.com

On air today: Dr. Fariba Karimi,
How to Start and Stop a Habit

Speaker	
Situation	
Topic	
Words and Phrases	

LISTEN

🔊 A. Listen to the podcast. Check (✓) if your predictions are correct or incorrect. For any that are incorrect, write the correct information.

	Correct	Incorrect	Correct Information
Speaker			
Situation			
Topic			
Words and Phrases			

🔊 B. Listen again. Complete the tasks.

1. Circle the gist of the interview.

　a. how to stop eating unhealthy food

　b. how to be less stressed at work

　c. how habits start and how to stop bad habits

　d. how to fix problems in our lives

2. Why do most people start bad habits?

　a. They are unhealthy.

　b. They have a problem.

　c. They can't talk to their boss.

C. Listen to the excerpts from the podcast. Choose the correct answer.

SECTION 1

1. What do we know about Dr. Fariba Karimi?

   a. She interviews people.

   b. She is a professor of psychology.

   c. She does not have any bad habits.

   d. She helps people with their problems.

2. What is a habit?

   a. a problem you cannot fix

   b. an activity we sometimes do

   c. something you often do without thinking

SECTION 2

3. Why do people start unhealthy habits?

   a. They don't sleep enough.

   b. They have a problem.

   c. They don't have anyone to talk to.

4. How does Dr. Karimi say most people feel about a problem?

   a. They don't want to think about it.

   b. They want to talk to someone about it.

   c. They don't know how to fix it.

5. When does an activity become a bad habit?

   a. when you don't want to stop it

   b. when you are stressed

   c. when you do it too much

SECTION 3

6. How do you break a bad habit?

   a. stop doing the habit

   b. try to fix the problem

   c. talk to your friends

7. Instead of doing bad habits, _____ .

   a. find a new problem

   b. start new, healthy habits

   c. talk about bad habits

LISTEN AGAIN

🔊 **A. Listen again. Check (✓) the habits Dr. Karimi talks about.**

☐ 1. eating too much

☐ 2. spending a lot of time on social media

☐ 3. exercising

☐ 4. eating healthy food

☐ 5. going to bed early

☐ 6. arriving late to meetings

☐ 7. playing too many video games

☐ 8. spending too much money

☐ 9. eating sweets

☐ 10. not sleeping enough

B. Read the statements. Circle *T* (true) or *F* (false). Correct the false statements.

T / F 1. A habit is something that you do often.

_____

T / F 2. Exercise and eating healthy food are examples of bad habits.

_____

T / F 3. Going to bed early is a good habit.

_____

T / F 4. A problem is usually the reason for a good habit.

_____

T / F 5. It is not possible to break a bad habit.

_____

C. What habits do you want to start? What habits do you want to stop? Write one example for each. Then walk around and interview three classmates. Write their habits in the chart. Use the example below to help you.

	I want to start ...	I want to stop ...
	going to the gym	*staying up late*
Me		
Classmate 1 **Name:**		
Classmate 2 **Name:**		
Classmate 3 **Name:**		

A: What habit do you want to start?

B: I want to stop _____ing.

A: What habit do you want to stop?

B: I want to stop _____ing. How about you?

VOCABULARY REVIEW

Complete the sentences with the words from the box.

become	enough	habits	possible	stressed
bored	fix	instead	spend	unhealthy

1. I always try to have good _____ , like eating healthy and going to bed early.

2. We _____ too much money on coffee.

3. Watching too much TV is _____ for you.

4. Giana always has something to do. She is never _____ .

5. I am _____ about my test, so I eat a lot of chocolate.

6. I eat junk food once a week. I don't want it to _____ a bad habit.

7. It is _____ to change your routine and break your bad habits.

8. Don't watch TV! Take a walk _____ .

9. There are so many problems at work. I don't think we can _____ them all.

10. I have _____ food. I don't want to eat too much.

○ Go to **MyEnglishLab** for more listening practice.

SPEAK

SKILL: MAKING AND RESPONDING TO SUGGESTIONS

A suggestion is an idea. We often make suggestions to help someone with a problem. For example, when a friend is sick, we can suggest resting or drinking tea. There are several ways to make suggestions.

These phrases are for making suggestions and responding to another person's suggestion.

Making Suggestions	Responding to Suggestions
You should …	That's a good idea.
Why don't you …?	Thank you. I'll try that.
How about _____ing?	Thanks for the suggestion.

GRAMMAR NOTE

Use the base form of the verb (the infinitive without *to*) after *You should …* and *Why don't you …?*

You should **sleep** more.   Why don't you **take** a walk?

Use the gerund (*-ing* form) with *How about …*

How about **eating** more vegetables?

🔊 **A. Listen to the conversation. Underline the expressions for making and responding to suggestions. Then practice the conversation with a partner.**

A: You're still playing video games?

B: Yes.

A: That's unhealthy. You should stop.

B: I know. But I'm bored.

A: Why don't you take a walk?

B: Thanks for the suggestion. But it's too hot outside.

A: OK. How about reading a book?

B: That's a good idea.

B. Think of a problem or bad habit you have (or someone you know has). Write it in the chart. In small groups, take turns talking about these bad habits or problems. Give one another helpful suggestions. Listen and write your classmates' habits and the group's suggestions in the chart.

Problem / Habit	Suggestions
Me:	
Classmate 1:	
Classmate 2:	
Classmate 3:	

Complete the sentences.

A suggestion is an _____ .

We make suggestions to help someone with a _____ .

Write three suggestions for a friend with a problem or a bad habit.

_____

_____

_____

_____

Grammar for Speaking Using *should* / *shouldn't* for suggestions

We use *should* and *shouldn't* (*should not*) to make suggestions or to give advice. *Should* has only one form.

Subject + *should* **+ base form of verb**

AFFIRMATIVE	NEGATIVE	QUESTIONS
I **should** go.	I **should not** / **shouldn't** go.	**Should** I talk to my boss?
You **should** eat healthy food.	You **should not** / **shouldn't** eat junk food.	What **should** I / he / she / we / they do?
We **should** study.	We **should not** / **shouldn't** spend too much money.	

A. Write the words and phrases in the correct order to form sentences.

1. spend / much / shouldn't / too / money / they

   _____.

2. on time / should / the / to / class / students / get

   _____.

3. a lot of / Sasha / eat / junk food / shouldn't

   _____.

4. when / Kristina / she / book / should / bored / is / read / a

   _____.

5. study / I / my / for / test / should

   _____.

B. Complete the conversations with *should* or *shouldn't*.

1. A: I want to be healthy.

   B: You _____ eat lots of vegetables.

2. A: I bought a new car.

   B: You _____ spend so much money.

3. A: Rei is tired.

   B: She _____ stay up so late.

4. A: Carla and David can't speak English well.

   B: They _____ study harder.

5. A: I don't feel well. I ate a lot of chocolate.

   B: You _____ eat a lot of sweets.

C. Write a suggestion to complete each sentence. Then practice the conversations with a partner. Use the example to help you.

   A: I have a test tomorrow.

   B: You should sleep enough tonight. / You shouldn't study all night.

1. A: I was late to class last week.

   B: _____

2. A: I want to go out tonight, but I don't want to spend money.

   B: _____

3. A: Susana is bored.

   B: _____

4. A: Martin and Thomas are stressed about the test.

   B: _____

5. A: I don't understand the homework.

   B: _____

6. A: My roommate plays her music too loud at night.

   B: _____

🔊 Go to **MyEnglishLab** for more grammar practice.

MAKE SUGGESTIONS FOR STUDY HABITS

STEP 1: LISTEN BEFORE YOU SPEAK

A. Look at the picture. Think about the speaker, the situation, and the topic. Then predict the words and phrases you will hear. Complete the chart.

Speaker	
Situation	
Topic	
Words and Phrases	

B. Review the words and definitions. You will hear these words in the conversation.

> **Glossary**
>
> **trouble:** problems that make something difficult
> **failing:** getting a bad grade in a class
> **course:** class at a university
> **daily:** happening every day
> **rest:** what is left after everything else has been used

C. Listen. Choose the correct answers.

1. What is the conversation about?

   a. how to change a course schedule

   b. how to exercise when you're busy

   c. how to find time to study

2. What is Elena's problem?

   a. She is failing two classes.

   b. She gets up too early.

   c. She watches TV in class.

3. What time does Elena wake up for her 9:30 A.M. class?

   a. 8:00

   b. 9:00

   c. 9:30

4. What does Elena do after class?

   a. She goes to the gym.   c. She studies at the library.

   b. She has lunch with friends.

5. What suggestions does the friend make? Check (✔) all that you hear.

☐ a. Get up earlier.   ☐ e. Go to the library after lunch.

☐ b. Eat a good breakfast.   ☐ f. Watch TV with friends.

☐ c. Study before class.   ☐ g. Go to bed early.

☐ d. Exercise before class.

D. Make another suggestion for Elena. What should she do? Write your idea. Then tell a partner.

_____

STEP 2: PREPARE TO SPEAK

A. Read the conversation. Underline all the suggestions. Then practice the conversation with a partner.

A: How are your classes, Elena?

B: Um … I'm having a little trouble. I'm failing two courses.

A: Oh, no! Why?

B: I'm too busy. I don't have enough time to study.

A: Really? What's your daily schedule?

B: Well, I get up around 9:00 A.M.

A: What time does your first class start?

B: 9:30.

A: You should get up earlier than 9:00!

B: Yes, you're right. I should get up earlier.

A: How about the rest of your day?

B: After class, I go to the gym. Then I go out to lunch with my friends. When I get back to the dorm, I relax and watch TV. After dinner, I study.

A: Well, there's the problem. You study at the end of the day. That's when you are tired.

B: Yes. That's true.

A: Why don't you get up early and exercise before class? Then how about going to the library to study after lunch?

B: That's a great idea.

A: You can watch TV after dinner. But you shouldn't stay up too late. You should go to bed early.

B: You're right. Thanks for the suggestions. I'll try them this week!

B. Read the list of bad habits related to school and studying. Add a few more ideas to the list.

eat unhealthy food	watch too much TV
don't exercise enough	play too many video games
go to bed too late	spend too much money
wake up too late	don't eat breakfast

My ideas: _____

_____

_____

C. Choose two bad habits from the list in Part B. Write suggestions for how to change the bad habits into good habits.

Bad Habits	Suggestions

STEP 3: SPEAK

Work in a group of four. Take turns saying your bad habits from Part C. Listen to your classmates' habits and make suggestions. Use the example to help you.

A: I have a bad habit.

B: What is it?

A: I _____ .

B: OK. I have a suggestion. You should … / Why don't you … ? / How about … ?

A: That's a good idea. / Thank you. I'll try that. / Thanks for the suggestion.

STEP 4: PEER FEEDBACK

Write your examples of bad habits from Part C. Listen to your group members' suggestions. Which ideas do you like the best?

Bad Habits	Classmates' Names	Suggestions

BUILDING VOCABULARY

RECOGNIZING AND USING -*ED* ADJECTIVES

Adjectives are words that describe something, for example, size, color, shape, style, personality. We can also use adjectives to describe how we feel. These adjectives add -*d* or -*ed* to the noun or verb form. Here are some examples of -*ed* adjectives.

Verb	Adjective	Examples
bore	bor**ed**	He is **bored**.
confuse	confus**ed**	The students were **confused**.
excite	excit**ed**	They are **excited**.
interest	interest**ed**	I am **interested**.
scare	scar**ed**	We are **scared**.
stress	stress**ed**	Sana is **stressed**.
surprise	surpris**ed**	I am **surprised**.
tire	tir**ed**	We are **tired**.
worry	worri**ed**	My parents are **worried**.

GRAMMAR NOTE

We use *to be* or *to feel* to describe feelings with -*ed* adjectives.

I am surprised.   He **feels tired.**   We **were worried.**

A. Write the -*ed* adjectives from the chart above under the matching pictures.

1. _____ 2. _____ 3. _____ 4. _____

5. _____ 6. _____ 7. _____ 8. _____

B. Complete each conversation with an -ed adjective from page 201. Then practice the conversations with a partner.

1. A: I don't understand these instructions.

   B: I agree. I am so _____ !

2. A: What grade did you get on the test?

   B: I got an A! I didn't study, so I was very _____ .

3. A: Why do you feel so _____ ?

   B: I have three exams tomorrow!

4. A: My parents are _____ about me. They think I only eat junk food at school.

   B: Well, they want you to be healthy.

5. A: Do you want to go to the photo club meeting?

   B: Yes, I am very _____ in photography.

6. A: I can't wait for the party on Saturday. It's going to be so much fun!

   B: I know! I'm so _____ .

7. A: I am so _____ ! There is nothing to do.

   B: Why don't we go to a movie.

8. A: I feel very _____ . I went to bed very late last night.

   B: You should go to bed early tonight.

9. A: I don't like that movie.

   B: I don't either. I was very _____ .

C. Discuss the questions with a partner.

1. Are you stressed about something? What is it? Explain.

2. What do you do when you are bored?

3. What hobbies are you interested in?

4. What are you excited about? A vacation? A course? A job?

5. What do you do when you are tired? Watch TV? Drink coffee? Take a nap? Take a walk?

◔ Go to **MyEnglishLab** to complete a vocabulary practice.

APPLY YOUR SKILLS

In this chapter, you listened to a podcast interview about how we start habits and how to stop bad habits. You listened to a friend make suggestions for how to find time to study. You gave suggestions for how to stop bad habits. In Apply Your Skills, you will listen to an interview with an author. You will give a presentation on your daily schedule and make suggestions to manage your time better.

VOCABULARY PREVIEW

A. Read the sentences. Look at the boldfaced words. Do you know what they mean? Share your ideas with a partner.

1. Good habits lead to **success**.

2. I want to **find** a good book to read.

3. It's important to exercise your body and your **mind**.

4. My **goals** are to get a job and spend less money.

5. I see one **mistake** on your test.

6. You need to practice **daily**.

7. I **prepare** for the day by writing a list of things I need to do.

8. I don't want to wait. Let's start **immediately**!

B. Write the boldfaced words from Part A next to their definitions.

_____ 1. the act of doing or getting what you want

_____ 2. things you want to do in the future

_____ 3. now; without waiting

_____ 4. every day

_____ 5. your brain, your thoughts, your way of thinking

_____ 6. look for and discover something

_____ 7. make something ready

_____ 8. something that is wrong or incorrect

Go to **MyEnglishLab** to complete a vocabulary practice.

PREDICT

Look at the pictures. Think about the speaker, the situation, and the topic. Then predict the words and phrases you will hear in the podcast. Complete the chart.

Speaker	
Situation	
Topic	
Words and Phrases	

LISTEN

A. Listen. Were your predictions correct? Which ones? Tell a partner.

My prediction was correct / incorrect about …

B. Circle the gist of the listening.

   a. suggestions for how to be successful

   b. suggestions for how to change a habit

   c. suggestions for how to learn a new skill

C. Listen to the excerpts. Complete the tasks.

SECTION 1

1. Abir Karim's book suggests _____ habits for success.

   a. seven

   b. ten

   c. eleven

2. Karim says that people should _____ .

   a. plan their day

   b. plan their evening

   c. wear something new each day

SECTION 2

3. Read the statements. Circle *T* (true) or *F* (false). Correct the false statements.

T / F   a. Karim says people can find one extra hour in the evening.

_____

T / F   b. Karim says people should get up very early every day.

_____

SECTION 3

4. Circle the correct word or phrase to complete the statements.

a. A suggestion Karim makes is to (**join an exercise group / learn something new**).

b. The host wants to (**take / teach**) piano lessons.

c. Karim says people (**should / shouldn't**) be scared of mistakes.

LISTEN AGAIN

A. Listen again. Circle the ideas the speaker talks about.

daily habits   learning new skills

breaking bad habits   listening to music

setting goals   avoiding mistakes

B. Number the habits in the order the speaker talks about them.

_____ learn something new

_____ set goals

_____ plan your day

_____ learn from your mistakes

_____ eat healthy food and exercise

_____ get up one hour early

C. Do you have any of the habits the speaker talks about? Write the ones you have. Then write your goals. Compare your habits and goals with three classmates.

Habit	Goal

I _____ . / I don't _____ .

My goal is to _____ .

VOCABULARY REVIEW

Complete the sentences with the words from the box.

daily	goal	mind	prepare
find	immediately	mistakes	success

1. I think _____ are good. They help us learn.

2. Oh, no! It's 5:15. We need to leave _____. I don't want to be late!

3. It's good to learn something new every day. _____ a topic you like and learn about it.

4. The semester was a _____. I learned a lot.

5. It takes a lot of work to learn a new habit. You need to practice _____.

6. Learning something new is good for your _____.

7. We should _____ for the trip this weekend. I want to be ready to go.

8. My _____ is to wake up early and go to bed early.

THINK VISUALLY

A. The two pie charts show how two types of people use their time. Look at the charts and answer the questions.

How People 25–54 Years Old with Children Use Their Time

1.8 hours · 8.6 hours · 1.2 hours · 1.1 hours · 1.1 hours · 2.6 hours · 7.6 hours

■ work ■ sleeping ■ free time / sports cleaning house
■ eating / drinking ■ caring for others ■ other

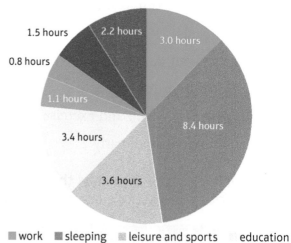

How College Students Use Their Time

1.5 hours · 2.2 hours · 3.0 hours · 0.8 hours · 1.1 hours · 8.4 hours · 3.4 hours · 3.6 hours

■ work ■ sleeping ■ leisure and sports education
■ eating / drinking ■ Personal ■ traveling ■ other

1. Who sleeps more?   ☐ a. 25- to 54-year-olds   ☐ b. college students

2. Who works more?   ☐ a. 25- to 54-year-olds   ☐ b. college students

3. Who travels more?   ☐ a. 25- to 54-year-olds   ☐ b. college students

4. Who has more free time?   ☐ a. 25- to 54-year-olds   ☐ b. college students

5. Who cares for others?   ☐ a. 25- to 54-year-olds   ☐ b. college students

B. Which graph is most like your schedule? How often do you do each of the activities? Tell a partner.

GRAMMAR

USING *SHOULD / SHOULDN'T* FOR SUGGESTIONS

A. Look at the charts in Think Visually. Write three suggestions for each type of person. Use *should* and the phrases you learned in this chapter. Use the example to help you.

College students should study more.

B. Read the habits. Think of a person in your life (family member, friend, roommate, yourself) who needs to start this habit. Then write a suggestion for that person. Use *should or shouldn't.* Use the example to help you.

My brother is lazy. He should exercise daily.

Habit	Person Who Should Learn the Habit	Suggestion
learn something new		
exercise		
set goals		
plan your day		
learn from mistakes		
eat healthy food		
wake up early		

ASSIGNMENT

Give a presentation about how you spend your time, and make suggestions for managing your time better.

PREPARE TO SPEAK

A. Think about your daily schedule. Complete the chart.

1. Write how much time you spend on the activity each day

2. Circle if you think it's OK or if you want to change it.

Activity	How much time	Comment
eating and drinking		OK Change
education		OK Change
leisure, sports, hobbies		OK Change
personal		OK Change
sleeping		OK Change
traveling		OK Change
other:		OK Change

B. Make a pie chart like the charts in Think Visually on the sheet of paper. Use your information from Part A.

C. Are you happy with how you spend your time? Do you want to make changes? What habits do you want to stop or start? Read the questions. Write your answers in the chart. Then share them with a group.

Questions	Answers
Are you happy with how you spend your time?	
Do you want to make changes?	
What bad habits do you want to stop?	
What good habits do you want to start?	
What other goals do you have?	

D. Practice your presentation. Use the sentence starters below. Remember to use *should* for your suggestions. Use the examples to help you.

I should …
I want to start _____ing _____.
I want to stop _____ing _____.
My goal is …

SPEAK

A. Give your presentation to your group.

B. Listen to your classmates' presentations. Write two classmates' names in the chart. Take notes on the habits or changes they talk about. Remember to ask for repetition or clarification when you don't understand.

Classmates' Names	Habits or Changes

Go to **MyEnglishLab** to complete grammar and vocabulary practices.

DEVELOP SOFT SKILLS

STUDYING FOR EXAMS

How do you feel when you have an exam? When, where, and how do you like to study? Everyone is different. But there are some good suggestions to help students be more successful. Starting to study early, getting a good night's sleep, using your notes to write a study guide, and joining a study group are a few examples.

Glossary

cram: try to remember a lot of information in a short time
depressed: very sad
review session: class meeting to review before an exam

A. Work with a partner or small group. Discuss the questions.

1. How do you study for an exam? Check (✓) the statements that are true for you. Write any other things you do.

☐ I study at home. ☐ I go to the library. ☐ I go to a coffee shop.

☐ I study alone. ☐ I study with a classmate. ☐ I study with a group.

☐ I read the textbook. ☐ I review my notes. ☐ I use my notes to write a study guide.

☐ I start to study long before the exam day. ☐ I cram the night before the exam. _____

A: How do you study for an exam?

B: I study with a classmate. I sometimes cram the night before the exam. How about you?

A: I study at home. I review my notes.

2. How do you usually feel before / during / after an exam? Complete the sentences with adjectives from the box, or use your own ideas. Then tell a partner.

I feel _____ before an exam.

I feel _____ during an exam.

I feel _____ after an exam.

bored	interested	worried
confused	scared	My idea: _____
depressed	surprised	My idea: _____
excited	tired	

🎧 **B. Listen to the conversation. Answer the questions.**

1. Why does Soyun feel happy?

_____

2. How did she study for the exam?

_____

3. How did Jiho do on the exam?

_____

4. How did he feel after the exam?

_____

5. What suggestion does Soyun make?

_____

C. Listen to the next part of the conversation. Check (✓) the suggestions that Soyun makes.

- ☐ 1. Take practice exams.
- ☐ 2. Don't cram.
- ☐ 3. Get a good night's sleep.
- ☐ 4. Make a list of questions to ask your teacher.
- ☐ 5. Start studying early.
- ☐ 6. Eat healthy snacks while you study.
- ☐ 7. Move around a lot.
- ☐ 8. Make a study guide.
- ☐ 9. Listen to music.
- ☐ 10. Make a graphic organizer.
- ☐ 11. Go to a review session.

D. Which of the suggestions in Part C are most useful for you? Which suggestions are not useful? Work with a partner. Practice making and responding to suggestions. Use the example to help you.

A: What's the best way to study for an exam?

B: You should listen to music while you study.

WHAT DID YOU LEARN?

Check (✓) the skills and vocabulary you learned. Circle the things you need to practice.

SKILLS

☐ I can ask for clarification and repetition.

☐ I can make and respond to suggestions.

☐ I can use *should* / *shouldn't* for suggestions.

☐ I can recognize and use *-ed* adjectives.

☐ I can study for exams.

VOCABULARY

☐ become	☐ find	☐ mistake	☐ surprised
☐ bored	☐ fix	☐ possible	☐ tired
☐ confused	☐ goal	☐ prepare	☐ trouble
☐ course	☐ habit	☐ rest (n)	☐ unhealthy
☐ daily	☐ immediately	☐ scared	☐ worried
☐ enough	☐ instead	☐ spend	
☐ excited	☐ interested	☐ stressed	
☐ fail	☐ mind	☐ success	

⬆ Go to **MyEnglishLab** to complete a self-assessment.

⬆ Go to **MyEnglishLab** for a challenge listening about Psychology.

Index

Toys "R" Us, 107⊕, 109
traits
    family, 55⊕
    personality, 55–57, 55⊕, 57t
Treasure Island, 6⊕, 7
trees
    in cities, 17–18, 17⊕, 48⊙
    in fight against climate change, 48⊙
twins studies, 99⊙

unhealthy habits, 191–193, 191⊕, 204⊕, 211⊙
United Arab Emirates (UAE), ideas of time in,
    178–179, 178⊕

V8 Hotel, 31–32, 31⊕
Venn diagrams, 155, 155f
verbs
    base form of, 195
    gerund form of, 195
    imperative, 141–143, 141t, 153
vertical gardens, 17–19, 17⊕, 19f, 48⊙
videoconferencing, 139⊙
virtual meetings, 139⊙
visual learners, 85⊕, 87, 87f, 97–99, 98t, 98⊕,
    99t
vocabulary learning strategies, graphic organizers
    in, 154–156, 154f, 155f, 156⊕

webs, word, 154, 154f
websites. *see* e-commerce; Internet
wh-words
    forming questions with, 10–11, 10t, 14, 14t,
        19
    in simple questions, 8–14
word maps, 155, 155f
words, making predictions about, 3–6
word webs, 154, 154f

Photo Credits